PROJECT ACHIEVEMENT:

Reading

P9-APC-189

George D. Spache, Ph.D.
Spache Educational Consultants

Evelyn B. Spache, Ed.D.
Spache Educational Consultants

And the Scholastic Editors

Scholastic Inc.

THE PROJECT ACHIEVEMENT STAFF

Project Editor: Jose T. Flores, Jr.

Reading Skills Researchers-Writers:
Mary F. Pomerleau, Suzanne Sayegh Thomas

Editorial, Production, Art Direction:
ZIGG-LYN Publishing Concepts & Services

Art Director: Jeff Fitschen

Design: Taurins Design Associates

Grateful acknowledgement is made to the following authors and publishers for the use of copyrighted materials. Every effort has been made to obtain permission to use previously published material. Any errors or omissions are unintentional.

Dudley Randall for the poem "Still Here" by Langston Hughes taken from the book, "The Black Poets," edited by Dudley Randall and published by Bantam Books, Inc. Copyright © 1971 by Dudley Randall.

Reader's Digest for adapted excerpts from "Is Your Child Taking Drugs?" condensed from "Beyond the Yellow Brick Road," by Bob Meehan with Stephen J. Meyer, July 1986. Copyright © 1986 by Reader's Digest Association, Inc.

USA Today for adapted excerpts from "It's Worse Than It Has been Before," by Mark Mayfield and Paul Clancy, May 16, 1986. Copyright © 1986.

Scholastic Update for adapted excerpts from "Stress Takes Its Toll," May 2, 1986. Copyright © 1986.

ISBN 0-590-34731-4

12 11 10 9 8 7   4 5/9

Contents

UNIT III
STUDY SKILLS ————————————————————————— 147

Introduction

The better you can read, the more easily you can get all the information you need to be successful in life. Here are four different ways that you can improve your reading *and* your test-taking skills.

1. By understanding the details in a reading passage.

Here is part of a reading passage you will find in this book. Read the passage and answer the question below it.

Richard Rutan, 48, and Jeana Yeager, 34, completed the first nonstop flight around the world on one load of fuel. They flew their experimental aircraft, the Voyager, 25,012 miles around the globe in nine days, three minutes and 44 seconds. This broke the records for distance flown without refueling and for endurance by aviators.

The Voyager has a canard shape, that is, the wing is at the rear of the plane and the stabilizer is near the front. Canard-shaped planes appear to be flying backwards. Voyager had two outriggers and two engines—a main engine at the back for cruising and an auxiliary engine in front for takeoff and landing. The featherweight plane, weighing 2,680 pounds when empty, was filled with fuel three times its weight—about 9,000 pounds or 1,500 gallons of aviation gasoline.

Choose the best answer.

With its full load of fuel, the Voyager weighed about __.
a. 2,680 pounds
b. 1,500 pounds
c. 9,000 pounds
d. 11,680 pounds

2. By figuring out what difficult words mean.

The words under **A** are from the passage above. Use clues from the passage to help you match each word with its meaning under **B**.

A	B
experimental	device for stability
aviators	trial
stabilizer	pilots
auxiliary	providing help

Find two more ways to improve your reading and test-taking skills on the next page.

3. By using visual materials, such as tables and graphs.

Study the table and answer the question below it.

WHERE PEOPLE FEEL GOOD					
	Satisfaction (10 = most satisfied)	Happiness (4 = very happy)		Satisfaction (10 = most satisfied)	Happiness (4 = very happy)
DENMARK	8.03	3.26 (5)	U.S.	7.57	3.26 (6)
SWEDEN	8.02	3.24 (8)	BRITAIN	7.52	3.33 (3)
SWITZERLAND	7.98	N.A.	BELGIUM	7.33	3.25 (7)
NORWAY	7.90	3.21 (9)	W. GERMANY	7.23	2.96 (13)
NETHERLANDS	7.77	3.30 (4)	FRANCE	6.63	3.09 (10)
N. IRELAND	7.77	3.34 (2)	SPAIN	6.60	2.98 (12)
IRELAND	7.76	3.36 (1)	ITALY	6.58	2.84 (15)
FINLAND	7.73	3.03 (11)	JAPAN	6.39	2.96 (14)

Which two countries have the least happy people? ___.

4. By recognizing the kinds of questions found on reading tests.

The experts say that there are many factors which affect a person's level of happiness. Among them are economic security, level of education, religious affiliation, and the sense of trust that a person shares with other people. We are told that anywhere in the world the happiest and most satisfied people share similar experiences. For instance, those who quit school before age 15 are the least satisfied people, and those who continue their education beyond age 20 are the happiest and the most satisfied.

Choose the best answer.

This passage is mainly about what makes people ___.
a. quit school
b. share similar experiences
c. happy and satisfied
d. decide to get married

Now you have practiced four kinds of reading and test-taking skills. You will find the same kinds of skills in the rest of this book.

Answers to exercises: 1. d; **2.** experimental—trial, aviators—pilots, stabilizer—device for stability, auxiliary—providing help; **3.** Italy and Japan; **4.** c.

UNIT I
READING COMPREHENSION

PART 1

Details and Main Idea

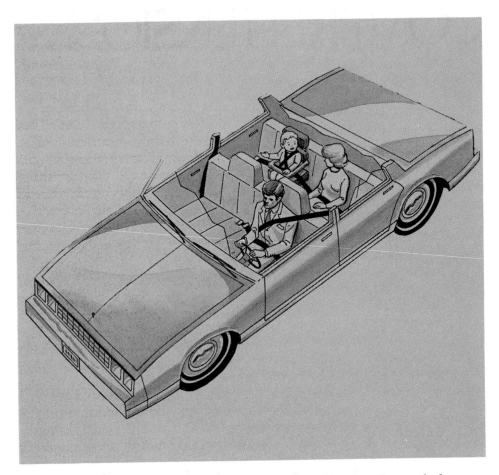

How many details can you find in this photo? The details can help you describe the photo's main idea.

In a reading passage, the details are any specifics such as names, dates, facts, directions, colors, and sizes. The main idea is a statement of what the passage is about. A statement of the main idea will not always be found in the passage. Sometimes, you must put together the details in the passage to find the main idea.

Almost all reading tests include questions about details and main ideas. The purpose of Part 1 is to help you learn how to answer questions about details and main ideas.

Find the details and the main idea in the following passage. Use the details to determine the main idea. Read the passage and answer the questions below.

Buckle Up!

When you buckle that seat belt, you become part of the car. When the car slows down, you slow down. If your seat belt isn't fastened, the car slows down but you don't. You keep going forward at the speed the car was going before it slowed down. You'll slow down too, when something hard stops your movement. That may be a real dead stop.

A seat belt also keeps you in the car. Ejection is responsible for about a third of all fatal accidents. "What if I'm trapped underwater or in a fire?" is a good question people have a right to ask. But being trapped doesn't happen very often. Even if it does happen, a seat belt may save you. It may prevent you from being thrown against the windshield, and may help you stay conscious. Conscious people are the only ones who are able to find a way out.

Choose the best answer for each question.

1. What happens when you fasten your seat belt?
   a. You get trapped in a fire.   c. Your body slows down.
   b. You become part of the car.   d. You hit a real dead stop.

2. According to the passage, about a third of fatal car accidents are caused by ___.
   a. getting trapped underwater   c. hitting the windshield
   b. ejection   d. driving fast

3. What is the best statement of the main idea of the passage?
   a. Seat belts can trap you in a car accident.
   b. A seat belt may help you stay conscious.
   c. You are safer in a car when you buckle up.
   d. You may slow down to a real dead stop.

Check your answers. You should have chosen **b** for 1, **b** for 2, and **c** for 3. Notice that in question 3, although answers **a, b,** and **d** are also true, they are only part of the main idea.

Find the details and the main idea in the next passage. Then complete the questions that follow. Each question has only one correct answer.

Reading For Pleasure and Profit

Did you ever sit down to read and find yourself daydreaming? Unfortunately, this is easy enough for most people to do. The challenge is to grab one's own attention and focus it on what must be read—an assignment, a user's manual, a warranty, a contract. But attention cannot be focused without some motivation.

Some students are motivated by a continual thirst for knowledge. Others are motivated by a desire for good grades. Most people are motivated by something particular and personal that relates to their own lives. These motives are not always subconscious or hidden. We can decide to be motivated. We can choose our own motive.

The first step in improving reading ability is to decide on a motive for reading a particular piece of printed matter. Are you reading for pleasure? For information? Out of curiosity? To achieve some goal? To make money? To avoid being cheated? To learn how to do a job?

If you are reading for pleasure, daydreaming is not a problem. You can read as rapidly as you wish. You do not have to note all the details.

If your motive is to find out some particular information, your motive and method are different. Assume you want to learn what kind of fuel is best for a certain model of car. You skim the pages of the manual until you find the information you are looking for. You focus your attention on the exact information you want.

Every motive for reading reflects personal needs and goals. It is important to focus on that motive, especially when reading to be informed more than to be entertained. Whether it's understanding how a complex machinery operates or if the customer wants a number 3 dish on the menu, focus on the motive for reading. It pays.

Choose the best answer for each question.

1. What does motivation mean?
   a. knowing something
   b. wanting something
   c. seeing something
   d. reading something

Check your answer. The passage says some people want knowledge, some want good grades, and some want pleasure. The correct answer is **b**.

2. According to the passage, the way to be motivated is __.
   a. to avoid napping
   b. to read for pleasure
   c. to decide to be motivated and to choose a motive
   d. to read critically

Check your answer. The passage clearly states at the end of the second paragraph that one must decide to be motivated and must choose a motive for reading. The correct answer is **c**.

3. Which of these is not a true statement about reading?
   a. Motives for reading are always subconscious.
   b. We do not read everything with the same skills.
   c. Reading at work and at the beach requires different motives.
   d. We sometimes read for details.

Check your answer. Details in the second paragraph indicate that motives for reading are not always subconscious, that they can be deliberately focused. The correct answer is **a**.

4. The passage is mainly about __.
   a. the first step in improving reading ability
   b. the first step in enjoying books
   c. reading for pleasure
   d. increasing reading speed

Check your answer. Review the details in the passage to determine the main idea. The main idea is a summary of what the entire passage is about. The correct answer is **a**.

Find the details and the main idea in the next passage. Complete the questions and then check your answers.

What Turns People On?

As you turn on your TV, you see a sleek red car and the rock star beside it says this is the car to drive. Switch the channel and you see striped toothpaste oozing out of a big blue tube. How do advertisers decide on what commercials can best make you want to buy their products? Not by guesswork, but by conducting studies on what turns most people on—what their values are.

Human values are like some "turn-on buttons." According to their studies, there are at least seven of these turn-on buttons:

Number-one button is money. Americans like to make and save money. This does not mean they are necessarily materialistic. Most people work hard to support themselves and their families. So, the idea of a sale or any other kind of bargain has instant appeal.

Number two is prestige. Everyone likes to feel important. We find beautiful cars, stunning clothes, and miracle cosmetics fascinating, especially if a media star is promoting them. Comfort or convenience ranks third. We want a phone in the car, remote control for the garage door or TV, a computer, a dishwasher—to make life easier. The other buttons are: health, security, family needs, and leisure. We want to feel younger and live longer, be secure in our homes, keep our family happy, relax and travel in our free time. Advertisers press these

buttons to turn people on and keep them buying. The next time you watch or read an advertisement, ask yourself if you really need the product. Keep in mind that some smart advertiser may just be pressing one of those buttons to convince you to part with your money.

Choose the best answer for each question.

1. Money motivates most people because __.
   a. people are greedy
   b. everyone loves sales
   c. money makes people feel important
   d. it takes money to live comfortably

2. Which is the second most important value to most people?
   a. leisure time   c. prestige
   b. health   d. wealth

3. Which of these is not listed as a top value?
   a. money   c. leisure time
   b. health   d. friendship

4. The passage is mainly about __.
   a. the human values that influence advertising
   b. ways to get rich
   c. TV commercials
   d. how consumers are fooled

Check your answers.

Question 1. Although there might be some people who are greedy and some who need money to feel important, the passage makes it clear that most people need money to live comfortably. The answer is **d**.

Question 2. Check back through the passage. It gives prestige as the second most important value. The answer is **c**.

Question 3. The importance of friendship is not discussed anywhere in the passage. The answer is **d**.

Question 4. Answer choice **b** is entirely wrong, answer choice **c** is not explicitly stated, and answer choice **d** is not even mentioned. The answer is **a**.

For lessons 3–8, look for the details and the main idea in each passage.

What Turns People Off?

Psychologists who advise advertisers on what turns most people on also tell us what turns people off. Number one is being ignored.

Have you ever been ignored by someone you like but who just doesn't seem to see or hear you when you say hello? Maybe you have been ignored by a teacher who calls on others no matter how much you wave your hand in the air. Or by a salesperson who looks through you and attends to someone else who may spend more money. Or by a friend you sent a gift to but who didn't even bother to reply.

Being ignored is the easiest turn-off to spot because it arouses immediate anger even in the mildest person.

Close to being ignored is being taken for granted. This turn-off may not be easy to recognize at once because it creates a more low-key resentment that builds up gradually. But taking people for granted makes them very angry. Did you ever have a teacher or parent who put up with lateness or laziness for weeks explode suddenly? Did you ever knock yourself out for someone, work hard to help, spent time and money—and get no appreciation? Instead, your extra effort is treated as if it was only what you were supposed to do. Another turn-off is negative criticism. Negative criticism is when you are told a real, hard truth about yourself or something you've done but you are not told anything to make you want to improve or to do better. When someone tells you "I really liked your hair a lot better the other way," that's negative criticism. If a friend of yours has written a story and you tell him only what you didn't like and nothing of what you liked about it, that is also negative criticism.

Being ignored, taken for granted, or negatively criticized makes you want to take revenge. But you can turn it around, instead. Try to be the kind of person who is interested in everybody and shows it. Never ignore people who go out of their way to communicate or interact with you. Listen to them when they talk to you, make them feel that what they say matters, that they matter. Acknowledge gifts, correspondences, gestures of courtesy, friendship and kindness. Say

"Nice job" to people who do decent work, and "Please" to those whose help you need. Say "I appreciate it" to anyone who has lent a helping hand, and smile and look that person in the eye when you say it!

Choose the best answer for each question.

1. According to the passage, people are "turned off" most by __.
   a. unkind remarks
   b. being taken for granted
   c. people with shifty eyes
   d. being ignored

2. Which of the following is a good way to ignore people?
   a. Write them thank-you notes.
   b. Call them by their right names.
   c. Let them know you know how hard they worked.
   d. Avoid looking at them.

3. Negative criticism is __.
   a. getting an answer backwards
   b. telling someone off
   c. criticism of disagreement
   d. criticism that tells a person the truth

4. The best way to avoid being ignored is to __.
   a. ignore those who ignore you
   b. take revenge
   c. go out of your way not to ignore others
   d. do something spectacular

5. Knowing what offends people is useful __.
   a. in all areas of life
   b. if you have a particularly unpleasant teacher
   c. primarily in the business world
   d. only on dates

6. Which sentence best describes someone being taken advantage of?
   a. I refuse to help out, unless I get something for it.
   b. I'd be glad to do it this once.
   c. I try to get others to do things for me.
   d. Somehow I spend all my time doing things for others.

Our Real Masters

You are a slave, just like the rest of us. You picked your own masters and told them, "Here, put the chains on me." Or, you may have said, "Make me the best I can be." Your real masters are your habits, and we all have them, either good or bad.

We don't decide anymore whether or not to brush our teeth in the morning—we just do it, it's a good habit. We don't stop at the head of the stairs and say, "Now what do I do with my feet to get down to the bottom?" Long ago, we picked up the habit of walking and it's part of us.

But there are some habits that do not help us or get us anywhere. Some of these habits begin as acts we do haphazardly and repeat until they become a pattern. Slouching, mumbling instead of speaking clearly, shuffling along, skipping meals, eating only junk food—all these can enslave us.

But the real tyrants are the mental habits. They're chains. Let's take Martha, for example. She is pretty but she doesn't think so. She has formed the habit of seeing herself as ugly. So, she doesn't bother to take care of her hair, or pick clothes that look good on her. "What's the use," she says to herself, "it won't make any difference." The habit of putting herself down is spoiling her life.

Jim has a habit, too. He's sure he can't learn to drive. Way back sometime, somebody told him he'd never make a good driver. Jim has forgotten who said it or when or why. He just formed the "I can't" habit and accepted the false idea that cars weren't for him.

How do you break chains like these? First, you have to want to break them. And then, you have to throw them away and replace them with *silver bracelets*. Martha's *silver bracelet* is a mirror, which she will look into every morning and say, "You're pretty, yes, you are pretty." Even if she doesn't believe it at first, she needs to hear it every day for herself. And when thinking pretty becomes a habit, she'll take care of her hair and pick clothes that will make her look pretty. And then someone will say she's pretty and she will believe it. Jim's *silver bracelet* will be "Hey, how about teaching me how to drive?" to someone he trusts. When he finds his hands on the steering wheel and hears "Great, you're doing great," his "I can't" habit won't be his master anymore.

Choose the best answer for each question.

1. Brushing your teeth is the same kind of habit as __.
   a. skipping meals
   b. being a poor driver
   c. eating the right food
   d. breaking chains

2. Which are the worst habits?
   a. mental ones, such as "I can't"
   b. diet ones, such as eating junk food
   c. automatic ones, such as walking
   d. physical ones, such as slouching

3. Substituting chains for *silver bracelets* means __.
   a. not being cheated
   b. replacing bad habits with good ones
   c. learning to wear becoming jewelry
   d. getting rid of all habits

4. According to the passage, in order to break the bad habit chains, you must first __.
   a. hear someone tell you how great you're doing
   b. think positive about yourself
   c. want to break them
   d. know what your bad habits are

5. What is the main idea of this article?
   a. Freedom can never be real.
   b. None of us is as good as we could be.
   c. A mirror can make you look pretty, if you keep saying you are.
   d. None of us is free of habits, but habits can be changed.

Your Creative Self

Remember the first time you brought a work of art home from kindergarten? Maybe it was a drawing of an Indian in a feathered headdress in front of his tepee. Someone looked at it and said, "Wow, that's beautiful! You're a real artist." Later on, someone might have said, "That's cute. What's it supposed to be?" All of a sudden you didn't see yourself as a great artist, and so you weren't.

According to Dr. William Beck of Basel, Switzerland, creativity is not a gift given to a chosen few. It is part of everyone's humanity. He believes that creativity is a learned process, one built on self-trust. Everyone is creative; everyone gets ideas. Some people trust their ideas and build on them. They scrape away the useless and elaborate on the good parts of the idea. Some, however, just drop their ideas.

Take, for example, the artist who sketches or paints. The artist is a person who trusts what his eyes say they are seeing, the shapes, the empty places, and the colors. When his brain says, "But every sky is either blue or gray, not pink," he just smiles and goes on with what his eyes see as true. And sometimes, as with Picasso and other modern artists, they know they are moving in new directions.

Then there are the musicians. Mozart knew he was great even if his contemporaries had their doubts. Writers, actors, and architects who have made important contributions to civilization had to endure the hostility before they heard the applause.

Scientists, too, are creative. They ask creative questions. Pasteur had to find out if tiny organisms like bacteria in milk were the cause of disease. If no one had wondered about how viruses could be used to prevent disease, smallpox, polio, and diphtheria would still be common deadly illnesses.

The problem for most of us, according to Dr. Beck, is waiting for the cheering section to show up. The creative person doesn't collapse when someone doesn't appreciate or understand his or her work.

They say schools stifle creativity, television stifles creativity, and critics stifle creativity. Nonsense. Our own egos stifle creativity and in the process also smother our dreams. So, go ahead and be creative in the ways you know you are. Don't wait for the cheerleaders and ignore the groaners. After all, what do they know?

Choose the best answer for each question.

1. The details build up to the main idea that __.
 a. people must believe in their own talents
 b. artists should be praised
 c. anyone can be a painter or musician
 d. scientists should be supported

2. The author got the information on creativity from __.
 a. a scientist in Germany
 b. a study made in American schools
 c. a Swiss doctor
 d. an artist's biography

3. According to the author, creative ability is required in __.
 a. art
 b. music
 c. science
 d. all areas of life

4. The article says the most creative people are __.
 a. the most intelligent people
 b. scientists who do research
 c. artists and musicians
 d. those who trust their own ideas

5. According to the author, what stifles creativity?
 a. our schools
 b. television
 c. critics
 d. our egos

6. The first step to creativity, according to the article, is __.
 a. getting ideas and asking questions
 b. trusting ideas to be worth investigating
 c. building on ideas
 d. adapting ideas to new situations

19

Young Entrepreneurs

A growing number of young entrepreneurs is shaking the business and educational world.

Steven Jobs is one of them. He was 22 years old when he founded Apple Computer. In one year, the company had revenues of almost two million dollars. In Georgia, then 24-year-old Xavier Roberts dreamed up a special kind of cuddly doll—the Cabbage Patch Doll—which became the rage of the 1980's.

Other young business tycoons include John Shorub, Kim Merrit, Joanne Marlow, Mark Hughes, and Barry Minkow. John started cutting lawns while still in the ninth grade. By the time he was 19, he owned Northwest Lawn Service and was making $152,000 a year. Kim, at 18, owned her own chocolate factory. Joanne, at 14, began designing clothes for her friends and at age 19 she had her own boutique. Mark founded Herbal Life at 23. Seven years later, he was grossing $512 million. Barry spent a lot of time thinking about spots on rugs. He got an idea for cleaning rugs and formed his own company. He named it ZZZZ-Best for a good reason. This way it was listed last in the phone book, making it easy for customers to find. That's about the only way his company was last. During the first year it grossed three million dollars. Recently, however, Barry was reported to have run into financial trouble and has been accused of fraudulent practices.

But on the whole, the motivation of these young tycoons was not primarily money. The prime goal must have been the implementation of a great idea. The concept of working for one's self was also important to these young entrepreneurs. They all agreed on these requirements for their success: a public need for the product or service, ability to set short and long-term goals, perseverance, an independent spirit, self-confidence, staying cool when things get rough or become uncertain, and the support of parents or someone who cares.

The schools are sitting up and taking notice. Many are inaugurating classes in practical economics at elementary and secondary levels. They are encouraging students to take business classes and join business clubs. Company executives are being invited into classrooms to share their knowledge and experience with the students.

Choose the best answer for each question.

1. Which paragraph contains the main idea?
   a. first
   b. second
   c. third
   d. fourth

2. According to the passage, which of these motivated the young people in putting up their businesses?
   a. money
   b. a great idea
   c. independence
   d. b and c

3. Which one of these is not given in the passage as a requirement for success?
   a. confidence
   b. perseverance
   c. money to invest
   d. ability to set goals

4. Schools have reacted to the success of the young entrepreneurs by __.
   a. dismissing them as freaks
   b. introducing classes in practical economics
   c. putting up companies of their own
   d. giving emphasis to money as a primary goal

5. An entrepreneur is __.
   a. a person who has a new idea
   b. a person who gets an idea off the ground
   c. a person who makes an idea work
   d. all of the above

6. The young entrepreneurs agree on how many requirements for their success?
   a. three
   b. four
   c. five
   d. seven

Applying For a Job—Looking Good!

In an interview between a Business Education teacher and the personnel director who interviews many young people for jobs in his company, the following ideas were explored. When asked about his first impressions of a candidate, the personnel director replied, "With all the commercials for soap, toothpaste, and deodorant, I would expect applicants to be clean. One indication of a person's ability is fingernails. Dirty fingernails on a man tell me he is probably careless. Dragon-lady fingernails on a girl tell me she is probably preoccupied with being glamorous. I don't need either quality in a worker."

The director went on to talk about clothes. "Job applicants should dress for the interview as they would for the job. A young man could wear a suit, or sport jacket with clean pants, a pressed shirt, shoes and socks. Girls should be dressed conservatively and avoid dangling earrings, too much makeup, tight sweaters, and see-through blouses."

Are there any other characteristics that the interviewer picks up when he first meets an applicant? "Absolutely," he said. "A person's

EMPLOYMENT OFFICE

carriage or posture tells me much about that person. If he or she shuffles in with the head down, that person probably won't work well with other people. An applicant who lounges in the chair is probably lazy. If the applicant stands with weight on one hip, I know the person has little energy and is going to lose interest fast."

"What I'm looking for," he concluded, "is someone who walks purposefully, stands straight until invited to be seated, and then sits, not plops. The person who gives the impression of being ambitious, hardworking and self-directed is the one I'm going to hire."

Choose the best answer for each question.

1. The basic impression an applicant should make is that of being __.
   a. charming
   b. attractive
   c. hardworking
   d. glamorous

2. According to the passage, what makes a bad impression during a job interview?
   a. skirts and blouses
   b. signs of carelessness
   c. earrings
   d. appearing ambitious

3. The interviewer is impressed by __.
   a. an applicant's appearance
   b. an applicant's attitude
   c. an applicant's background
   d. a and b

4. Which of the following personality traits makes a bad impression during a job interview?
   a. shyness
   b. ambition
   c. alertness
   d. self-confidence

5. Dressing for the job interview means __.
   a. looking like a fashion model
   b. wearing anything but blue jeans
   c. dressing conservatively
   d. wearing gloves

6. Which of the following states the main idea of the passage?
   a. A job applicant's appearance creates a strong first impression.
   b. Talent is more important than appearance.
   c. Appearance is the only thing that counts in a job interview.
   d. Interviewers have a good sense of fashion.

Applying For a Job—Mind Your Manners!

Job interviewers are looking at more than an applicant's appearance. They are also looking for personality traits that indicate the applicant's ability to succeed on the job. "Applicants should look interested," said the interviewer. "After all, I have to decide in 15 or 20 minutes of observation and conversation if this person is mature enough, healthy enough, honest enough, and energetic enough to work for us." When asked what would be a favorable sign that the candidate is acceptable, the interviewer replied, "Manners. An applicant's manners give away a great deal about that person."

"For instance," she went on, "does the applicant know enough to wait to be asked to be seated? To shake hands only if I offer mine? To introduce himself or herself and to speak clearly? To look me in the eye? Is the applicant on time for the interview? Does he or she say 'Thank you' after the interview?"

"Some of the negative things applicants do are smoke, chew gum, crack knuckles, and pick at nail polish." She told a story of another interviewer who drops a book when a male candidate comes in for an interview. "If the fellow automatically stoops down to pick it up for him, the interviewer knows that the applicant is instinctively courteous."

To some people, the interviewer's acceptable standards may be too excessive. But the job market is filled with young men and women

seeking employment. Job applicants should be realistic about their opportunities. They must realize that going for an interview is really a selling job. They are selling themselves as people who are more competent, more industrious, and more talented than any of the other applicants. Getting hired is really making the sale.

Choose the best answer for each question.

1. According to the passage, what would the interviewer consider bad manners in an applicant?
   a. saying "Thank you"
   b. introducing himself
   c. asking questions
   d. being late for the interview

2. What would the interviewer consider good manners?
   a. speaking clearly
   b. shaking hands immediately
   c. complaining about being kept waiting
   d. standing during the whole interview

3. What judgment does the interviewer not have to make?
   a. if the applicant is hardworking
   b. if the applicant is honest
   c. if the applicant is healthy
   d. if the applicant is going steady

4. Which is not a desirable facial expression for a job interview?
   a. annoyance   c. disinterestedness
   b. boredom   d. all of these

5. According to the passage, what makes a bad impression on an interviewer?
   a. talking about oneself
   b. shaking hands with the interviewer
   c. smoking while being interviewed
   d. appearing interested in the job

6. Which advice states the main idea of the passage?
   a. Don't be shy.   c. Be courteous.
   b. Say "Thank you."   d. Be kind to job interviewers.

Find the details and the main idea in each reading passage on the next four pages. Read the test tips before you read each passage. Put the answers to the questions on your answer sheet.

Test Tips: Watch for main-idea questions that ask you to choose a title for a passage. Most reading passages on tests have no titles.

A group of parents in New York State drew up a list of books they considered offensive to Jews and Christians or simply "filthy." A Long Island school board removed some of the listed books from the school libraries. These included Kurt Vonnegut's *Slaughterhouse Five*, Bernard Malamud's *The Fixer*, Eldridge Cleaver's *Soul On Ice*, and Langston Hughes' anthology of *The Best Short Stories by Negro Writers*.

Students sued the school board for violating their First Amendment right to free speech—and by extension, their right to free inquiry.

The case reached the Supreme Court in 1982. The high tribunal asked the lower court to examine the school board's reasons for removing the books. The Supreme Court ruled that a school board may ban books which it considers unsuitable for children, but not simply because the books express unpopular political views. The case was dismissed when the school board returned the books to the libraries.

1. Students sued the school board for violating their __.
   a. agreement
   b. right to free inquiry
   c. school policy
   d. library rules

2. The case was dismissed after the __.
   a. students demonstrated
   b. school board returned the books to the libraries
   c. students withdrew their suit
   d. parents tore up their list of banned books

3. The Supreme Court ruled a school board may not ban books simply because the books express __.
   a. unpopular political views
   b. religious ideas
   c. communist doctrines
   d. unfounded theories

4. Which is the best title for the passage?
   a. "Banned Books"
   b. "Censorship in Schools?"
   c. "School Board Sued"
   d. "Filthy Books"

What picture comes immediately to your mind when you think of the U.S. Constitution? Probably, a rolled-up scroll or printed pages?

James MacGregor Burns, a political scientist in Massachusetts, thinks of another image. The Constitution, he says, is like a fancy Swiss watch —the mechanical kind with lots of dials and stop-and-go buttons.

Burns says the Constitution is a complex mechanism which has its balances, power and controls, just like a watch whose insides are balanced and have springs which give it the power to move at a correct speed. Powers and limitations of those powers are properly apportioned among the three separate branches of government—the executive, the legislative and the judiciary. By letting the three branches of government check each other, the Constitution stops any one branch from becoming too powerful.

The Constitution is always ticking away, performing most of its functions out of sight like a good watch. It protects your rights, nurtures technological innovation and even helps keep foods safe for you to eat.

5. Burns says the Constitution and a Swiss watch both __.
a. always run smoothly
b. were created by experts
c. have balances and controls
d. are priceless

6. The Constitution allows the three branches of government to __.
a. be completely independent
b. check each other
c. abuse their powers
d. ignore each other

7. The best title for the passage is __.
a. "Watches At Work"
b. "Checks and Balances"
c. "Limits to Power"
d. "The Highest Law"

8. The Constitution __.
a. is not complex
b. does not function
c. limits government powers
d. favors the executive branch

9. James MacGregor Burns is a __.
a. government official
b. senior college student
c. political scientist
d. well-known historian

Test Tips: Try each answer choice with the question before you choose
the best one.

In 1901, President Theodore Roosevelt authorized "The White
House" as the official name for the home of the President of the
United States. It contains the living quarters of the president and his
family and the offices for conducting official business.

It has become one of the most popular tourist attractions in the
country. More than one million visitors a year go through the White
House to look at the rooms that are open to the public every day from
10 A.M. until noon except Sunday, Monday, and holidays. On the first
floor in the East Wing, opposite the Executive Wing, are five elegant
rooms: the State Dining Room, the Red Room, the Blue Room, the
Green Room, and the East Room.

The State Dining Room is where the president's official banquets are
held. The Red Room, Blue Room, and Green Room are parlors where
the president entertains guests. The East Room, in gold and white, is
the largest room in the White House. It is 79 feet by 36 feet and is
used to entertain guests after formal dinners. The first family, guests
and staff occupy most of the 127 other rooms in this beautiful mansion.

---

10. How many rooms are in the
    White House?
    a. 127   c. 190
    b. 132   d. 1,901

11. Tourists may visit the White
    House daily except __.
    a. Monday   c. holidays
    b. Sunday   d. a, b, and c

12. The East Room is __.
    a. never used by the president
    b. used on formal occasions
    c. the smaller room of the
       White House
    d. used by the president's
       family and guests

13. The passage is mainly
    about __.
    a. what tourists can see at the
       White House
    b. where the name White
       House came from
    c. the president's quarters
    d. the White House offices

14. Which of these are not in the
    White House?
    a. government offices
    b. the president's home
    c. rooms for staff and guests
    d. courtrooms

Test Tips: Some reading tests have passages with words missing. If you understand the passage, you will know the missing words. Six words are missing from the passage on this page. First, read the entire passage to learn the main idea, and keep the main idea in mind. Then, look at each numbered item below the passage. Decide which of the four details is the best choice to complete the corresponding blank.

One day in 1977, United States President Jimmy Carter noticed an awful _15_ in the White House. He quickly discovered its source: a mouse had crawled into an Oval Office wall and died there. Carter was about to _16_ a foreign diplomat, so an aide asked the General Services Administration (GSA) to remove the mouse immediately. But GSA officials insisted they had already killed all the mice inside the mansion. They said the dead mouse must have come from the White House grounds which were being maintained by the Department of Interior. The aide contacted Interior officials who then said they were _17_ only for federal lands, not for dead mice indoors. Fuming mad, Carter summoned the GSA and Interior officials to his smelly office. "I can't even get a dead mouse out of my office," complained the chief executive of the most powerful _18_ in the world.

Putting their heads together, the officials agreed on a _19_. They created an inter-agency task force to be supervised by the White House in removing one single dead mouse from the office of the president!

Most presidents have told similarly bizarre stories about coping with the U.S. civil service but for the most part, the civil service has won the battles. A president can issue orders but his directives must follow _20_ laid down by the civil service.

15. a. truth   c. story
    b. smell   d. sight

16. a. call   c. receive
    b. appoint   d. greet

17. a. responsible c. penalized
    b. neglectful d. negotiating

18. a. nation   c. business
    b. weapon   d. army

19. a. debate   c. reconciliation
    b. strategy   d. price

20. a. guidelines c. wishes
    b. complaints d. directions

PART 2

Inference

Some people created and placed on display the masks in this photo. What was their purpose? The details in the photo can help you figure out the answer. The parts you see can help you to make an inference about what you don't see.

Making an inference in your reading means finding the meaning when it is not actually stated. Reading materials contain a lot of details. You won't always have to remember the details, but you will need to understand what they mean. One way to do that is to think about the details and how they relate to each other.

On reading tests, many questions ask for answers that are not stated in the passage. The purpose of Part 2 is to help you answer those kinds of questions.

The questions following the selection ask for inferences. Think about the details in the selection to determine the answers to the questions.

Why Are You the Way You Are?

All parents—whether human beings, animals or plants—pass down certain traits to their offspring. This process is called heredity.

Human beings inherit not only physical but mental traits as well. Among the physical traits are general build, the color of skin, eyes, hair, and the shape and size of nose, ears, hands, and feet. Among the mental traits are the ability to learn and enhance talent in fields such as science, mechanics, art, and music.

Each offspring gets 23 chromosomes from each parent. Within each chromosome are pairs of genes. One of them is dominant and the other recessive or weaker. So if your eyes are blue, it means that the gene for blue eyes from one of your parents was the dominant gene and the gene for brown eyes from your other parent was the weaker gene.

Human traits are also greatly influenced by the environment. The conditions of your surroundings—your home, your parents, friends, teachers and other people in your community—can influence and make a difference in, or change your life.

Choose the best answer for each question.

1. A person's personality is apparently influenced by __.
    a. the genes of parents   c. science and medicine
    b. the environment   d. both a and b

2. The author of the passage probably based his writing on a __.
    a. news story   c. political column
    b. scientific paper   d. human-interest news feature

3. The author apparently wants to stress the source of a person's __.
    a. intelligence   c. good looks
    b. traits   d. talent

Check your answers. You should have chosen **d** for 1, **b** for 2, and **b** for 3. The words *apparently* and *probably* indicate inference questions. If you missed any of the questions, review the details in the selection and make the correct inferences.

LESSON 1

Making inference has been an enlightening and entertaining mental task for centuries. The earliest writing in Old English is full of riddles or details from which you were to infer the meaning. The riddles were preserved by scholars who were living in Britain 1,300 years ago. Their riddles covered a wide range of everyday subjects like food, birds, animals, the sea, weapons, and the weather. Here is an example of a type of riddle they loved. Read it carefully and answer the questions below.

1 I devour the snow.
   The ice struggles against me.
3 It pours itself down in tears.
   Together we move the ships down to the sea.
5 The worms love me.
   The green buds greet me.
7 Some nights I am fierce and tear at your door.
   Some days I am gentle and tap on your roof.
9 I am a thief, but I am generous.
   Who am I?

Choose the best answer for each question.

1. If green buds greet the speaker, it is probably ___.
  a. summer   c. fall
  b. winter   d. spring

Check your answer. The word *probably* shows you that you will need to make an inference by using details in the selection. Plants *bud* in the springtime. The correct answer is **d**.

2. If ice becomes tears, it ___.
  a. cries   c. freezes
  b. melts   d. piles up

Check your answer. Details in the selection suggest that the ice is melting. There are no details about anything crying or freezing or piling up. The correct answer is **b**.

3. The speaker may steal, but also is generous in giving ___.
  a. life through the wind
  b. green buds to the trees
  c. life to the earth
  d. boats a way to the sea

Check your answer. Details in *Lines 5* and *6* suggest that the speaker nourishes the earth. The answer is **c**.

4. If the speaker is sometimes fierce and sometimes gentle, you infer it is ___.
  a. a woman
  b. a storm
  c. seawater
  d. the spring rain

Check your answer. Details in *Lines 1, 7,* and *8* suggest that the speaker is the spring rain which melts the snow, tears at the door, and taps on the roof. The answer is **d**.

LESSON 2

The poet expresses his thoughts and feelings through pictures (images) in the mind which the words and rhythm create. One of America's greatest poets, Robert Frost, heightened the use of the ordinary in both language and imagery.

The Road Not Taken

Two roads diverged in a yellow wood
And sorry I could not travel both
And be one traveler, long I stood
And looked down one as far as I could
To where it bent in the undergrowth;

Then took the other, as just as fair,
And having perhaps the better claim,
Because it was grassy and wanted wear;
Though as for that the passing there
Had worn them really about the same,

And both that morning equally lay
In leaves no step had trodden black.
Oh, I kept the first for another day!
Yet knowing how way leads on to way,
I doubted if I should ever come back.

I shall be telling this with a sigh
Somewhere ages and ages hence:
Two roads diverged in a wood, and I—
I took the one less traveled by,
And that has made all the difference.

Robert Frost

Choose the best answer for each question.

1. In deciding which road to take, it is apparent the poet __.
  a. found it easy to decide
  b. found it difficult to decide
  c. refused to decide
  d. postponed his decision

2. The road the poet took was __.
  a. narrower   c. more worn
  b. wider   d. not used as much

3. The leaves in the wood were __.
  a. green   c. yellow
  b. black   d. brown

4. From what he says in the third stanza, the poet will probably __.
  a. return to take the other road
  b. not return to take the other road
  c. not care about returning
  d. regret taking the road he followed

5. By the end of the poem, the poet is probably satisfied because __.
  a. he expects a great future
  b. other choices will come his way
  c. he took the less traveled road
  d. he has a chance to take the other road

Check your answers.

Question 1: Before deciding which road to take the poet stood long and looked down far as he could. The answer is **b.**

Question 2: The poet describes the second road as grassy and wanting wear. The answer is **d.**

Question 3: The poet refers to a "yellow wood." You should have chosen **c.**

Question 4: Doubt is expressed by the poet about returning to take the other road. The correct answer is **b.**

Question 5: In the last stanza, the poet says that traveling the less traveled road made all the difference. The answer is **c.**

LESSON 3

For lessons 3 through 12, infer from the details in the selection to answer the questions that follow.

"The Ultimate Field Trip"

On January 28, 1986, the space ship Challenger exploded and fell into the ocean just after takeoff. Among the seven astronauts on board was Christa McAuliffe who was to be the first "private citizen" to fly in space. She was selected by NASA, the National Aeronautics and Space Administration, from among 10,000 school teachers who applied for the honor.

She was born Sharon Christa Corrigan on September 2, 1948. She grew up in Framingham, near Boston. She played softball, went to movies, and did things other kids all over the U.S. did. She went to college in Framingham and taught school in Maryland. She married Steven McAuliffe who became a lawyer. They moved to Concord, New Hampshire, where they had two children, Scott who was nine at the time of the tragedy and Caroline who was six. Christa taught Social Studies in Concord High School.

The two lessons that she planned to teach from outer space were to be called "The Ultimate Field Trip" and "Where We've Been, Where We're Going. Why?" The first was to be a tour of the shuttle and an explanation of the jobs of the six other members of the crew. The second was to be about why we explore space, what we have learned, and what we hope to learn from future space projects. This lesson was to use several experiments to show how liquids and solids react differently in space from the way they react on earth. For example, oil and water on Earth mix and then separate. In space they stay mixed. Solids, like marshmallows and heavier candy like m&m's in a plastic bag, would mix. On earth, the heavier candy would fall to the bottom of the bag. In space, because of weightlessness, solids of varying weight would not separate.

Most Americans were in shock as they watched on television "the ultimate field trip" Christa McAuliffe and the other six astronauts took into eternity. The public was so caught up in the idea of an ordinary person going into space that very few Americans anticipated the catastrophe. And unexpectedly, instead of being opposed to the idea of further space exploration, most Americans are determined to support the government's plan to pursue the conquest of the limitless space frontier.

Choose the best answer for each question.

1. The title has two meanings. One has to do with the space flight itself. The other probably refers to the flight __.
   a. as a sad one for Americans
   b. as a final one for the seven astronauts
   c. being shorter than planned
   d. an incredible spectacle

2. Christa McAuliffe was probably chosen to represent the private citizens because of __.
   a. her courage
   b. her ordinary background
   c. her familiar profession
   d. all of these

3. Christa McAuliffe was not __.
   a. from a small town
   b. family oriented
   c. a high school teacher
   d. certified in math and science

4. The lessons that Christa planned to send to Earth were probably __.
   a. aimed at high school students
   b. designed for adults
   c. too complicated
   d. meant for the general public

5. One of Christa's lessons was designed to __.
   a. demonstrate the difficulty of space travel
   b. explain how a space shuttle works
   c. show how candy can be eaten in outer space
   d. explain how each astronaut contributes to the mission

6. Many Americans probably feel that __.
   a. space is too dangerous for travel
   b. Christa should have stayed in the classroom
   c. outer space is still a frontier to be explored
   d. astronauts take too many chances

LESSON 4

The Ultimate Aviation Flight

Flying around the world is no big deal these days. All you have to do is buy the necessary airline tickets to circle the globe. But to fly around the world without landing and without refueling, that's a record-breaking feat.

This is what two American pilots did in December 1986. Richard Rutan, 48, and Jeana Yeager, 34, completed the first nonstop flight around the world on one load of fuel. They flew their experimental aircraft, the Voyager, 25,012 miles around the globe in nine days, three minutes and 44 seconds. This broke the records for distance flown without refueling and for endurance by aviators of such a flight. The last existing distance flight record was 12,532 miles set by Air Force pilots in a specially modified B-52 in 1962.

Dick Rutan's younger brother, Burt Rutan, 43, designed the experimental Voyager. The plane had a canard shape, that is, the wing is at the rear of the plane and the horizontal stabilizer is near the front. The plane of the Wright brothers also had a canard configuration. Canard-shaped planes appear to be flying backwards. Voyager had two outriggers and two engines—a main engine at the back for cruising and an auxiliary engine in front for takeoff and landing. The featherweight plane, weighing 2,680 pounds when empty, was filled with fuel three times its weight—about 9,000 pounds or 1,500 gallons of fuel. Almost all parts of the plane were filled with fuel—the main wings, outrigger booms, canard wing, and fuselage. When the plane landed on December 23, 1986 at Edwards Air Force Base in California, where it took off nine days earlier, only five gallons of fuel were left. Its average speed was 115 mph.

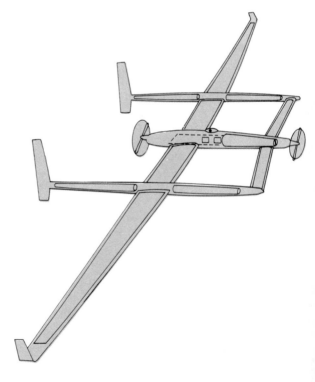

The Voyager's radical design is expected to bring changes to how planes are built in the future. Military aircraft and cargo planes are expected to benefit from the Voyager's success.

The whole project—completed in six years—was the handiwork of a group of volunteers, with no government support. President Ronald Reagan awarded the two pioneering pilots with the Presidential Citizens Medal.

Dick Rutan, at the end of the flight, told a news conference, "In America, people are free and can do whatever they want to do, as long as they dream it. This is the last first in aviation."

Choose the best answer for each question.

1. Voyager's featherweight design was apparently intended to __.
   a. make sure it could survive bad weather
   b. enable the plane to carry as much fuel for the nonstop flight
   c. make it fly faster
   d. impress the government

2. Richard Rutan and Jeana Yeager are apparently good __.
   a. plane designers   c. in business
   b. pilots   d. in aviation technology

3. The success of the Voyager will probably bring changes in __.
   a. military plane designs   c. space vehicle designs
   b. commercial plane designs d. a and b

4. The government awarded the two pilots with the Presidential Citizens medal to __.
   a. make up for not supporting them in their project
   b. give due recognition to their pioneering achievement
   c. officially confirm the record set
   d. encourage them to break their own record

5. The Voyager was described as an experimental plane because __.
   a. it had two engines   c. it had a canard shape
   b. it flew longer than other planes   d. it had a radical design

6. The success of the Voyager apparently was cheered by __.
   a. Americans only   c. plane designers
   b. aviators   d. the whole world

Science City

The Japanese have a talent for taking the inventions of other people and carrying them to a level of excellence. But they have realized that they must also take the initiative in the world of science and technology. To do this, they have developed Tsukuba Science City, a beautiful suburban-like city 37 miles from the huge, overcrowded, and bustling city of Tokyo.

Tsukuba is a planned community devoted to science and engineering progress. The living areas are at the center, and there is a plan to accommodate 200,000 people, although only half of that number live there now. Central to the concept of the community is its school system. Tsukuba officials believe that the very strict educational policies and the rote learning of the traditional Japanese school system do not encourage questioning or challenging, and curiosity, or creativity. Japanese students have invariably followed an intense discipline of taking detailed notes, memorizing them, and then repeating them on examinations. The University of Tsukuba operates differently. An applicant's extracurricular activities and outside interests as well as examination scores are used as criteria for admission. In the Tsukuba classroom, as at the best American universities, professors encourage discussion and questioning.

The fields of research being explored in this city are biology, agriculture, science, engineering, construction, and higher education and training. The classrooms are housed in five groups of institutes with one group having common facilities to serve all fields. This is to encourage scientists to work together and share their knowledge instead of competing with each other. At the opposite end of the city from the university are the Institutes for National Research and Disaster Prevention, and the National Laboratory for High Energy Physics. It is in these institutes that scientists study the frequent earthquakes (about 1,500 a year) that plague Japan. In the Building Research Institutes, huge buildings have been erected and shaken apart to study the effects of earthquakes on different types of architecture.

In 1985, Japan staged an Expo to show off the city and make it popular among its own people. About $2.5 billion was spent for this exhibition. The fair is over. Now, are the Japanese people willing to leave the advantages of a city like Tokyo, to move to the suburbs and participate in this exciting world of exploring the possibilities of science? That remains to be seen.

Choose the best answer for each question.

1. The Japanese city is probably ___.
   a. very modern
   b. very clean
   c. very efficient
   d. all of these

2. The Japanese probably admire American education for its ___.
   a. emphasis on grades
   b. thoroughness
   c. lack of examinations
   d. encouragement of class discussion

3. The traditional Japanese education probably does not encourage ___.
   a. creativity
   b. ingenuity
   c. competitiveness
   d. all of these

4. The author seems to feel that Tsukuba ___.
   a. makes education too easy
   b. offers courses that are too difficult to pass
   c. has much to offer its students and the Japanese people
   d. is too concerned with agricultural research

5. The research on earthquakes is probably done at Tsukuba because ___.
   a. the necessary talent and space are there
   b. earthquakes occur frequently in the area
   c. earthquake research is popular with students
   d. the government pays for it

6. The Japanese people are probably slow to accept Tsukuba because ___.
   a. they like the prestige of the old universities
   b. they enjoy living in large cities like Tokyo
   c. Tsukuba is not a beautiful city
   d. a and b

LESSON 6

Monster Man

Walking into Roy Knyrim's basement can be pretty scary if you don't know him. Roy is in the monster-making business. He has been making monsters since he was 10 years old. That's when he sent for a book called "Movie Monsters and How to Make Them." Then Roy got a professional make-up kit and he has been making monsters ever since. His dream is to become a make-up effects artist in the movie industry.

Going to job interviews, Roy gets into trouble sometimes. When his suitcase went through an airport X-ray machine, the machine operators saw the outlines of the monster heads he was carrying and Roy had to take them out to show the operators the heads weren't for real. Sometimes Roy tries his creations on strangers, to see how close to real he has made his special effects. "I'd go to a carnival with a fake hand," explains Roy. "Then I'd take it to the top of the Ferris wheel and drop it, and the people below would scream."

Roy doesn't know where his monster-making ideas come from. While his ideas are his own, he admits being a fan of Stephen King, whose horror stories are best-sellers.

Some of Roy's creations are mechanical. The monsters' eyes and mouths move, making them more realistic.

His family has learned to live with his unusual career. "It's weird, but great," says his brother Kurt, adding "but it can be scary walking into the basement in the middle of the night."

Choose the best answer for each question.

1. When Roy first decided to make monster-making a career, his family probably ___.
   a. welcomed it immediately
   b. felt uneasy about it
   c. were indifferent about it
   d. gave him monster-making books

2. Visitors wandering into Roy's basement probably were ___.
   a. surprised   c. scared
   b. happy   d. unaffected

3. Roy wants to pursue monster-making because ___.
   a. it scares people to death
   b. it makes a lot of money
   c. he enjoys the job
   d. he hates the job

4. How did Roy test his special effects on strangers?
   a. by rolling a head down the aisle of a movie house
   b. by dropping a fake hand from a Ferris wheel
   c. by pulling strangers into his basement
   d. by doing all of the above

5. When Roy was ten years old, he probably ___.
   a. was easily scared by horror stories
   b. preferred reading poems
   c. was not scared by horror stories
   d. did not read comic books

6. Roy wants to work in the movie industry probably because ___.
   a. more horror movies are being filmed today
   b. he will meet others who also make monsters
   c. he will be able to fully develop his talent
   d. he will make millions of dollars

Rock History

Many people connect rock music with the young and the restless. However, it has been around for about 40 years. Beginning in the late 1940's as "rock and roll," it probably got its name from a hit song like "Good Rockin' Tonight."

In 1956, a country singer with an electric guitar who combined western music with black rhythm and blues in a song called "Heartbreak Hotel" made rock and roll music famous. Elvis Presley continued to produce hit records, to star in 33 movies, and to become a national idol.

As television became a primary entertainment medium, radio stations emphasized the role of the disc jockey. It was they who pushed rock music, and its popularity soared. Bill Haley and the Comets was the first rock band to be famous. Chuck Berry, a black blues singer and composer, influenced rock and roll by getting away from sentimental songs like "Love Me Tender" and writing music which focused on the problems of youth. The Kingston Trio and Bob Dylan sang "serious rock" music in the 1960's with emphasis on civil rights, political dissent, and poverty. The Beatles brought from Britain a new rhythm combined with witty lyrics to create another form of rock. In the 1970's, rock operettas like "Hair" and "Jesus Christ Superstar" reflected the wide entertainment appeal of this music.

By the late 1970's, however, protest music lost ground and blues became the focus. Loud and energetic music like "Heavy Metal," as well as songs with meaningful lyrics written by Paul Simon and James Taylor became popular. Discos combined Latin rhythms and catchy blues music in popular dance tunes.

In the 1980's, the production of videos which combine acting, dancing, visuals, sound and lighting effects with music became popular. Michael Jackson's "Thriller" in 1983 was a monumental success.

Today, rock music is inspired by a sense of social justice as artists like Bruce Springsteen use their talents to raise money for the poor and the unemployed. Music, then, has become more than sound. It has become a medium for spreading ideas and values which can deeply affect the way we think and behave.

Choose the best answer for each question.

1. Elvis Presley probably __.
   a. had a major effect on rock music
   b. influenced jazz music
   c. surprised everyone by his popularity
   d. was just lucky

2. Apparently, radio disk jockeys __.
   a. tried to kill rock
   b. gave rock its first wide audience
   c. had little to say about what the stations played
   d. were musicians themselves

3. The rock music of the 1960's was probably __.
   a. a reflection of the times
   b. a new form of music
   c. not popular with youths
   d. affected by television

4. In giving only brief mention to the various rock groups, it is apparent that the author __.
   a. has no knowledge about these groups
   b. dislikes their music
   c. felt they should be written about in separate articles
   d. gives more importance to the music and its history

5. There is apparently room in rock music for __.
   a. great variety
   b. little diversity
   c. no changes
   d. a few new stars

6. Rock music will probably __.
   a. die out in the next 10 years
   b. give place to classical music
   c. be forgotten quickly
   d. move in new directions

Copyrighting Songs

Ever since Raynos Tayler registered "The Kentucky Volunteer" with the U.S. Copyright Office in 1794, Americans have been seeking to copyright their songs. Tayler's song was about a boy going off to fight American Indians. Today's tunes cover everything from commercials to love songs. Songs are written on paper napkins, scraps of cardboard, yellow lined paper, but most of them are recorded on cassettes. About 125,000 offerings appear each year. They come from punk bands, individuals, and even prisoners such as Charles Manson. They also come from judges like the late Supreme Court Justice, William O. Douglas.

To copyright a song, all that is needed is $10 and the answers to a two-page questionnaire. The lyrics must be original. They must be heard clearly above the music, running water, crying baby, or whatever is in the background. And they must be substantial enough to suit the reviewers. The song "Ooh, ahh" was not granted a copyright. But titles can be wild, and become wildly successful. For example, "Yes We Have No Bananas" in the 1920's and "Dead Skunk" from the 1970's were both hit songs.

If the writer is granted a copyright, ownership lasts for life and for 50 years after death.

Choose the best answer for each question.

1. Copyrighting is apparently intended to protect the rights of __.
   a. the public
   b. the author
   c. the U.S. Copyright Office
   d. radio stations

2. The requirements of the copyright office are apparently __.
   a. very strict
   b. complex
   c. easy and simple
   d. useless

3. Lyrics are required to be original probably to prevent __.
   a. theft of someone else's song
   b. listeners from being bored
   c. confusion among reviewers
   d. pile up of applications

4. The copyright law apparently protects the author's rights for __.
   a. a very short time
   b. ten years only
   c. 50 years
   d. life

46

Treasure Hunter

Mel Fisher read *Treasure Island* by Robert Louis Stevenson when he was a youth in Indiana. He loved the idea of treasure-hunting. In 1985, at the age of 65, he loved it even more. That was the year he found the *Nuestra,* a Spanish ship which sank in the 17th century off the coast of Key West, Florida. The treasure he found after 16 years of searching, was worth $40 million!

Some people who were not involved in the search claimed they were entitled to part of the treasure. The Supreme Court, however, ruled that since Mel had over 1,000 investors who financed his long search, only they and Mel could claim a share of the booty. The ship was laden with gold, silver, emeralds, and other wonderful relics of 17th-century Spain. Some artifacts were donated to the Key West Museum.

Mel Fisher gets enormous satisfaction in watching history come alive for young people. When they see a true relic of the Spanish Empire in a gold coin or in an emerald ring, he knows that this may heighten their understanding of a distant time and place.

Choose the best answer for each question.

1. Of Mel Fisher's discovery of the *Nuestra,* the writer is apparently __.
   a. skeptical   c. not interested
   b. thrilled   d. surprised

2. The people who wanted part of the booty may have been __.
   a. Florida officials   c. the Spanish government
   b. museum officials   d. all of these

3. The Supreme Court decision implies that Mel Fisher __.
   a. was greedy   c. was lazy
   b. had an honest claim   d. was obligated to Spain

4. If Mel supported his investors' rights, what would this imply?
   a. He has pride.   c. He is a good businessman.
   b. He is dishonest.   d. He is honest.

5. Apparently, Mel Fisher enjoys __.
   a. watching children learn   c. investing his money
   b. going to museums   d. reading Treasure Island

Monkey Business

When Sue Strong was 20 years old, she was injured in a car accident which left her a *quadriplegic,* that is, a person who is paralyzed from the neck down. She found that her most difficult battle was against the depression which was brought on by her dependency on other people for such simple things as pouring a glass of water, or changing a cassette tape. That is, until Henrietta arrived.

Mary Joan Willard at the Albert Einstein College of Medicine in New York City has been developing ways of training capuchin monkeys to assist the handicapped. One of her students, Henrietta, is a lively six-pound monkey. She is like the ones seen with *organ grinders* or street musicians, which is trained to work with the handicapped the way a "seeing eye" dog is trained to work with the blind. She lives with Sue in her Manhattan apartment and prepares lunch, changes books and cassette tapes for her, and turns the lights on and off at her command.

To direct Henrietta's activities, Sue's motorized wheelchair is rigged with a device which she manipulates with her chin. It points a red laser dot at an object in the room and Henrietta performs a task connected with the dot such as closing a door, or getting a soda from the refrigerator and inserting a straw in it.

Not only is Henrietta amazingly intelligent, but she is also fiercely loyal. When Sue returned from a two-week vacation, Henrietta went wild with joy. She hugged Sue and chattered away for hours. Sue is convinced that Henrietta was trying to tell her how horrible her life back at the lab was.

Ordinarily, though, Henrietta demonstrates her affection for Sue more quietly. She sits on her lap and grooms Sue's arms and toes. If Henrietta is near enough, Sue moves her right arm and rests it on the monkey's little body. That gesture tells Henrietta that she's loved and appreciated.

Sue explains that Henrietta views affection in the same way a normal person would. When Henrietta loves, she expects to be loved in return.

Choose the best answer for each question.

1. Which of these would a capuchin monkey probably not be able to do?
   a. turn off the lights
   b. put a straw into a glass
   c. give medicine
   d. comb hair

2. The primary value of using monkeys to assist the handicapped is that ___.
   a. it appeals to the handicapped person's caring instincts
   b. it gives the handicapped a sense of independence
   c. it gives these special monkeys good homes
   d. it allows the handicapped to develop many skills

3. The word *fiercely* as used in this selection means ___.
   a. savagely
   b. violently
   c. intensely
   d. cruelly

4. Capuchin monkeys probably cannot ___.
   a. respond to lasers
   b. relate to people who can walk
   c. serve liquids
   d. maneuver motorized wheelchairs

5. According to the selection, Henrietta ___.
   a. causes many problems for Sue
   b. is capable of performing several tasks
   c. is unable to handle food
   d. is as intelligent as any human

6. Is it likely that monkeys will replace human assistance to the handicapped?
   a. Yes, because few people want to work with the handicapped.
   b. Yes, because monkeys are cheaper than paying support personnel.
   c. No, because monkeys are difficult to train.
   d. No, because a monkey's role in aiding the handicapped is limited.

LESSON 10

The State of Many Firsts

Alphabetically, Wisconsin is listed next to the last among the states. But it is a state which has lived up to its motto, "Forward", and has through the years come up with many firsts.

Consider all these firsts: direct primary elections, pensions for teachers, minimum wage laws, and workmen's compensation. It was the first to have kindergarten classes, to use numbers to mark highways, to require safety belts on cars purchased in the state, and to have vocational schools and schools for training teachers. Wisconsin also was the first state to abolish the death penalty.

Wisconsin is known also as "America's Dairyland." About 40% of the nation's cheese and about 25% of the country's butter come from there. Thousands of dairy cattle graze on its green, rolling pastures. However, an even greater portion of the state's wealth comes from manufacturing. Wisconsin is the nation's leading producer of engines and turbines. Wisconsin factories also manufacture electric machinery, household appliances, and automobiles. They can peas, corn, and other vegetables and make the metal cans as well as cutlery and hardware. They brew more beer than any other state.

Its many lakes also make Wisconsin a great recreation area for summer sailing and winter ice boating. Its beautiful forests create a vacation land for hundreds of hunters, campers, hikers and horseback riders. These same forests also make Wisconsin home to the paper industry.

Choose the best answer for each question.

1. According to the passage, Wisconsin is apparently __.
   a. ordinary   c. backward
   b. progressive   d. conservative

2. The people of Wisconsin are apparently __.
   a. lazy   c. industrious
   b. healthy   d. weak

3. The state of Wisconsin adopted "Forward" as its motto probably to __.
   a. impress others
   b. inspire its people to progress
   c. have a short motto
   d. be different from others

4. The author apparently __.
   a. is impressed by Wisconsin's progress
   b. is not interested in living in Wisconsin
   c. does not like any other state
   d. has not seen any other state

5. Wisconsin will probably__.
   a. lose its industries
   b. try to be more progressive
   c. be content with what it has already achieved so far
   d. change its motto

6. Wisconsin's lakes and forests apparently attract a lot of __.
   a. businessmen
   b. animals
   c. vacationists
   d. students

The American Dream State

Beautiful smiling girls with flowers in their hair bringing leis of orchids; clear, crystal blue waves breaking white on warm beaches; surfers laughing against an incredible rose-and-gold sunset; iridescent peach and purple flowers blooming in a dark-green rain forest. Those are the dreams that are making Hawaii the number one vacation choice of many Americans. But the dreams only hint at the beauty to be found in this fascinating island.

There is the climate. Statistics show that the average temperature is 77 degrees with a variation up or down of only 5 degrees. On the island of Hawaii itself, there are dry areas where as little as 10 inches of rain a year fall. It is there that magnificent new resorts are located. On the northeast side of the island, as much as 300 inches of rain fall on the mountains and on the Akaka Falls, cascading from 442 feet above a wooded grove.

The soft white beaches blending into clear turquoise waters are a major attraction. There are also black sand beaches with glistening grains of lava. There are volcanos like Mauna Loa and Kilauea which are breathtaking, but not dangerous. They are located in the Hawaii Volcanos National Park. Visitors can drive through a rift in one of them and stand on the edge of a crater to look down into the fire pit which, according to legend, is the home of the goddess Pele.

Hawaii offers tourists much to do. In addition to sight-seeing among the natural beauties, there are small towns and sugar cane plantations to visit. Swimming, sailing, diving, deep-sea fishing, hiking, and horseback riding are some of the more popular sports. Pageants, parades and feasts take place almost every month of the year.

Finally, there are the warm and welcoming Hawaiian people. Their ancestors came from Europe, Japan, the Philippines, China, and Samoa. Those who are regarded as native Hawaiians are descendants from the Polynesians who first settled in the land. In fact, the living descendants of King Kamehameha, like Princess Kawananakoa, represent the only royal family in the United States.

Choose the best answer for each question.

1. The figures on Hawaii's annual rainfall apparently came from the __.
   a. hotel managers
   b. weather statistics
   c. television stations
   d. tourists

2. The volcanos are considered not dangerous probably because __.
   a. they do not erupt during the tourist season
   b. they are located in a national park visited by many tourists
   c. the government has learned to control them
   d. they have harmed only a few people

3. The kind of tourist who would best enjoy Hawaii is probably someone who __.
   a. likes only water sports
   b. enjoys visiting castles
   c. is not afraid of volcanos
   d. wants a variety of activities

4. Hawaii's history is apparently __.
   a. not interesting   c. long and varied
   b. very brief   d. unknown

5. Hawaii's climate is apparently__.
   a. hot   c. rainy
   b. mostly good weather   d. cold

6. The Polynesians probably traveled to Hawaii by __.
   a. plane   c. boat
   b. walking   d. swimming

LESSON 12

Below is a translation of an Eskimo story on survival in the land of ice and snow that is Alaska. Carefully note the details in making inferences.

Survival

One bad winter when everyone was weak with hunger
And the village decided to move to new hunting grounds,
Arfek had to leave behind his old mother-in-law Kigtak
To crawl over the ice and catch up if she could.
It was a pitiful sight and we did not laugh
For it probably meant death for her:
The old lady was half blind and crippled
And she was not wearing enough clothes for the weather
But as long as she could crawl she followed:
Life was still sweet to her.
No one here among us wishes to harm old people
For we ourselves might live to be old someday,
But Arfek had no choice but to leave Old Kigtak behind.
He couldn't let her ride on the sledge,
For he had only two dogs, and as it was
He and his wife had to help drag the sledge, weak as they were.
He couldn't go back to get her after they camped
Because that would mean spending the night
Traveling back and forth
When he had to be at the breathing holes
Early next morning to hunt for food.
He could not allow his wife and children to starve:
He had to think of them first
For they had their lives ahead of them,
Rather than help an old, worn-out woman
Who was at death's door anyway.

54

We have a custom that old people who cannot work anymore
Should help death to take them.
Old Kigtak thought of this, left behind, all alone on the ice.
She knew she was useless and couldn't work anymore,
So why hang on as a burden to her children?

You see, it is not that we have hard hearts
But the conditions of life here are merciless
And to survive in a land of ice and snow
Sometimes we must be without pity.

Choose the best answer for each question.

1. The story is mainly about __.
   a. hunting in Alaska
   b. the Eskimo family life
   c. survival under harsh conditions
   d. Alaska's weather

2. The villagers decided to leave their old place apparently because __.
   a. they wanted a change of environment
   b. they wanted to get rid of the old people
   c. they could no longer find food there
   d. they wanted to go to a warmer climate

3. In leaving his mother-in-law behind, Arfek probably felt __.
   a. proud
   b. angry
   c. sad
   d. disgusted

4. We can infer from the story that __.
   a. Eskimos have no compassion
   b. Eskimos show greater wisdom regarding old people
   c. Eskimos are very brave
   d. Eskimo life is very different from ours

5. From the details in the story, "breathing holes" apparently means a place where __.
   a. Eskimos catch their breath
   b. Eskimo families sit around to tell stories
   c. polar bears drink
   d. sea mammals, like seals, come up for air

6. Old Kigtak kept struggling to catch up probably because __.
   a. she was sure she could make it
   b. her desire to live is very strong
   c. she wanted to say goodbye to her children
   d. she knew they would return for her

7. According to the story, old people among Eskimos should __.
   a. try to live long if they could
   b. help death to take them
   c. always stay healthy
   d. go to other places

8. Because of the conditions of life in his land, Arfek apparently had to think first of __.
   a. himself
   b. his mother-in-law
   c. his wife and children
   d. his dogs

TAKING TESTS

Practice making inferences from details in each reading selection on the next three pages. Read the test tips before you read each selection. Put your answers to the questions on your answer sheet.

Test Tips: On a test, try reading the questions before you read the selection. Then you will know which details to concentrate on.

Alaska was once called "Seward's Folly." It was bought from Russia in 1867 by then Secretary of State William Seward for $7 million. People considered it just a wasteland of ice and snow.

Alaska is more than twice the size of Texas. It has 591,004 square miles, but only 68 persons for every 100 square miles. It is often called the last frontier because it is still so unpopulated. Most of the people live in cities like Anchorage and the capital city, Juneau.

There is a wide range of temperatures, and the summer sun shines 20 hours a day. That makes it possible to farm there. Farmers grow potatoes, barley, and raise livestock. They also raise greenhouse and nursery products. The country is wealthy in fish. It is rich in minerals and timber. Oil is also a great source of Alaska's wealth.

There are airstrips that make it possible to reach even the most remote Eskimos. Communication stations are scattered all over the state to help protect America from invasion. They make Alaska a different kind of "frontier," only 50 miles from Russia.

"Seward's Folly" may have been a great buy after all.

---

1. Alaska today is apparently __.
   a. still nothing but a wasteland
   b. being developed rapidly
   c. progressing very slowly
   d. highly populated

2. Because of its closeness to Russia, Alaska today __.
   a. protects the United States from invasion
   b. encourages invasion
   c. increases communication with Russia
   d. makes America weaker

3. At the time he bought Alaska, Seward apparently became __.
   a. unpopular   c. rich
   b. more powerful d. poor

4. The people who opposed Seward's purchase of Alaska would probably __.
   a. feel the same way today
   b. not care about it today
   c. admit Secretary Seward did right
   d. oppose it even more today

Test Tips: As you read the passage, decide on a word that would probably fit in each blank. Then see if one of the answer choices with each number below the passage matches your choice.

The Cajun French of South Louisiana are known for their spicy hot dishes, including gumbo, jambalaya, red beans and rice, pork roast and boiled crawfish. On Saturday nights, they dance to the music of the fiddle and accordion and sing folksongs that are immensely _5_ in the region.

This fun-loving people have a proud history. They are _6_ of the 17th-century French colonists who settled in Acadia, Canada, now the province of Nova Scotia. Fiercely proud of their language and their Catholic faith, their ancestors defied the English who gained control of Canada under the Treaty of Utretch in 1713. The French settlers _7_ to take an oath of allegiance to the English king and to accept the Church of England as their church. They also refused to fight against their Indian neighbors for the English.

In 1775, they were _8_ from Acadia, forced into ships that took them to American seaports like New York, Philadelphia, and Savannah. Eventually some of them migrated to Louisiana, where there were many other French Catholics, as well as German and Spanish _9_. They intermarried, so their descendants often have family names that do not sound French. A culture emerged that was called Acadian. This name got shortened and slurred until it became known as Cajun.

Throughout the past 200 years, they have amassed a rich _10_ of oral tradition, folklore, music, dance, and culinary arts. Their French language has remained at the heart of their culture. It is a dialect comprised of the 17th-century Acadian French and many words assimilated from their Spanish and Indian neighbors.

---

5. a. unknown   c. noisy
   b. popular   d. hated

6. a. ancestors   c. descendants
   b. enemies   d. friends

7. a. refused   c. agreed
   b. loved   d. conspired

8. a. emigrated   c. immigrated
   b. debarked   d. deported

9. a. natives   c. settlers
   b. invaders   d. foreigners

10. a. heritage   c. wealth
   b. code   d. legend

Test Tips: Many tests contain poems. Use the details in the poems to figure out the meanings of the poems. Sometimes the lines are numbered to help you answer the questions.

Some literary critics consider Langston Hughes (1901–1967) to be the foremost modern black poet. The poem below is an example of his use of the black urban or rural dialect. Read the poem aloud and note the peculiar spellings and pronunciations used.

1 I been scarred and battered.
  My hopes the wind done scattered.
3   Snow has friz me,
  Sun has baked me,
5 Looks like between 'em they done
  Tried to make me
7 Stop laughin', stop lovin', stop livin'—
  But I don't care!
9   I'm still here!

Still Here by *Langston Hughes*

---

11. The poet feels that life is __.
    a. too easy
    b. full of natural wonders
    c. real hard but to be alive is worth it
    d. completely hopeless

12. In *Line 2*, the poet means that ___.
    a. winds depress him
    b. he lost hope because of a storm
    c. his dreams are lost because of hard times
    d. a strong wind changed his plans for the day

13. In *Lines 3* and *4*, the poet conveys the feeling of __.
    a. indifference   c. hope
    b. helplessness   d. victory

14. The poet uses words like *"friz"* (frozen) and other forms of slang because __.
    a. he is not a good speller
    b. he is trying to be funny
    c. he wants to heighten the poem's meaning
    d. he wants to be different

15. In *Line 9*, the poet is probably __ to live his life.
    a. convinced   c. afraid
    b. determined   d. trying

The people in this photo are expressing a stand against a social menace. What is their opinion? How do they express it? What is the purpose of their gathering?

When you read an article, the same kinds of questions are important. What is the purpose of the article? What opinions are given, and how are they supported? Thinking about such questions as you read is called *critical reading*.

Most reading tests include questions about the opinions in an article, and the reasons why the article was written. The purpose of Part 3 is to help you learn to answer those kinds of questions.

Before you begin to answer the questions following the article, ask yourself: Who might have written this? Why? What is the writer's opinion? Is the opinion supported? Do I agree with or object to it?

Garbage In, Garbage Out

Next to fire and the wheel, reading is probably the most useful tool man has discovered or invented. Fire which warms us can also burn the house down. The wheel can carry us to our death. Reading can be far more dangerous because it is a tool of the mind.

There is a lot of garbage in print that influences the lives of people. Everything that people take into their mind somehow becomes part of them. Gulping down garbage from a garbage dump would surely make us sick. So can mental garbage get stuck in the conscious and subconscious mind and lead us to thoughts and actions that can hurt and destroy others.

Think about what you read. Value your own opinion. You have a right to accept or reject what you read in the newspapers, in magazines and books, and what you hear or see on the electronic media. Remember that if garbage comes in, it is only garbage that will come out.

Choose the best answer for each question.

1. The main purpose of the article is to warn against reading __.
   a. excessively
   b. habits
   c. trashy material
   d. about fire and accidents

2. The author believes that reading __ our thoughts and actions.
   a. is more important than
   b. can influence
   c. puts trash in
   d. should not influence

3. According to the article, in reading something, a person must __.
   a. agree with the opinion of the writer without question
   b. value his own opinion on what he has read
   c. treat everything he reads equally
   d. let others decide for him

Check your answers. You should have chosen **c** for 1, **b** for 2 and **b** for 3. If you missed any of the correct answers, check the details in the article.

Read the following article and answer the questions on the next page.

Illiteracy Breeds Crime

Illiteracy and poverty are major roots of crime. If a city marks its map to show the section where 75% of the people do not finish high school, where illiteracy is above 15%, where health is poor, and where the per capita income is 60% of the city as a whole, it is also marking the section with the highest crime rate.

Judge Clementine Barthold, Superior Court judge in Jefferson County, Indiana, is among those who made this conclusion after many years of involvement in helping juvenile offenders. She found out that illiterate kids are frustrated kids who eventually got into serious trouble. She organized juvenile care centers, group counseling for young offenders and their parents, tutoring and community service forms of punishment long before such approaches became common.

Judge Michael Farrell also believes illiteracy is a major cause of crime. He advises young people to "Read and thumb the dictionary!" His own experience taught him that poverty itself is not the problem and that education prevents crime. When he came to the U.S. at the age of 16, he had only one dollar in his pocket. He came from Ireland where higher education was forbidden him and he had to be taught secretly by the parish priest. When his application for admission was turned down by a major American University, he found a way to learn Latin, Greek and Philosophy. He became a lawyer and then a judge and devoted himself to counseling immigrants to the U.S. He also served on a local school board, helping to upgrade the education of poor and displaced people.

Both Judge Barthold and Judge Farrell are advocates of preventing crime among the youth through education.

A young person convicted of a crime and sent to prison learns the ways of the criminal world and struggles to survive in that world. Many others like Judge Barthold and Judge Farrell believe that first offenders, and those who seem willing to learn, can be reformed. It is time to try forms of rehabilitation that are practical and geared toward teaching law offenders how to change their behavior for the better. Once reformed, they can become productive members of their communities.

Choose the best answer for each question.

1. Where would this article probably appear?
   a. on the front page of a newspaper
   b. in a popular magazine
   c. in an encyclopedia
   d. in a history book

Check your answer. When you can identify what kind of passage you are reading, you are practicing critical-reading skills. Think about your experiences with the materials listed in all the answer choices. The answer is **b.**

2. This article was written mainly ___.
   a. to argue against prison reform
   b. to argue in favor of preventing criminal behavior
   c. to offer sympathy for criminals
   d. to show where the most crimes in a city occur

Check your answer. If you know the main idea of the article, you will know the author's purpose in writing it. The correct answer is **b.**

3. The two judges cited in the article agree that crime would be greatly reduced if ___.
   a. all criminals were released
   b. capital punishment was abolished
   c. criminals were never released
   d. young people were not illiterate

Check your answer. Test each of the answer choices before choosing the best one. From the details in the passage, you know that answer choices **a** and **c** are obviously false. Answer choice **b** is not discussed in the article. The correct answer is **d.**

4. Which of the following opinions would the author agree with?
   a. Little good will come from rehabilitation.
   b. Criminals have to be taught new ways of behaving.
   c. Society will never benefit from former criminals.
   d. Criminals have little chance of ever being good citizens.

Check your answer. Reviewing details in the passage will prove that the author would not agree with answer choices **a, c,** and **d.** The correct answer is **b.**

Read the following passage. Use the details to answer the questions. Then check your answers.

Kicking the Drug Habit

In his book, "Beyond the Yellow Brick Road," Bob Meehan writes about his experience with drugs and how he kicked the drug habit. For ten years he took all forms of drugs and robbed people to support the habit. He spent three years behind bars. When he finally kicked the drug habit, he founded a drug abuse program and has shown thousands of teenagers and their parents how to beat the drug problem.

What made him decide to turn his back on drugs? "I found a better way to live," he writes. During the 16 years he has worked with drug dependents, Meehan has pinpointed three crucial steps that drug addicts should take on the road to recovery.

First of all, the addicts must admit that they themselves are to blame for the mess they're in. Drug abusers, according to Meehan, have a remarkable ability to rationalize their behavior. They blame others for the problems they themselves create. The first important step to recovery is for the drug abusers to stop looking at themselves as the victims of other people and recognize that they are the victims of drugs. Once they have decided to kick the habit, the addicts should protect themselves by sticking with people who do not take drugs.

It may take from one year to 18 months before a recovering drug addict may be strong enough to rejoin our "get high" society. Meehan advises that a former drug abuser should always have sober people around who can provide him or her the necessary support.

A third vital step is for the addict to believe in some higher power and turn their will and life to that Higher Power. "The support of other people—positive peer pressure—is what recovering drug abusers need more than anything else when they decide to go straight. The support of others is *love*—which is what God is," concludes Meehan.

Choose the best answer for each question.

1. This article is aimed at ___.
    a. making parents aware of the drug crisis
    b. helping drug addicts kick the habit
    c. enlisting teachers in the antidrug campaign
    d. getting government support for the antidrug campaign

2. According to author Meehan, the first step a drug addict should take in kicking the drug habit is to ___.
    a. rationalize his behavior   c. admit responsibility
    b. blame others for his problem   d. depend on others

3. Why did author Meehan decide to quit drug dependency?
    a. Because he was jailed for it.
    b. He found being sober a better way to live.
    c. He wanted to put up a drug abuse program.
    d. He outgrew the habit.

4. What does a drug abuser need most to quit the habit?
    a. medicines   c. money
    b. support of other people   d. a vacation

Check your answers.

Question 1. Answer choices **a, c,** and **d** may be part of the author's purpose, but his main objective is stated in answer choice **b.**

Question 2. Review the details in the third paragraph. Answer choices **a** and **b** are incorrect. Answer choice **d** is partly true. The correct answer is **c.**

Question 3. Answer choices **a, c,** and **d** are reasonable. Review the details in the second paragraph. The best answer is **b.**

Question 4. Answer choices **a, c,** and **d** are only partly true. Details in the last paragraph support answer choice **b** as the correct answer.

LESSON 3

Read the selections in lessons 3 through 7. Practice your critical-reading skills by using details to answer the questions that follow each selection.

Growing Up In Basketball

Unlike a lot of American kids, basketball professional star Patrick Ewing didn't grow up playing the game. As a child in Jamaica, Pat knew nothing about the sport. In fact, he never shot a ball at a hoop until he was 12 years old.

High school coach Mike Javis recalls the first time he saw Pat Ewing play. It was right after the boy's family moved from Jamaica to Cambridge, Massachusetts.

"He was big and tall," says Javis, "but if you asked me then what it would take to turn him into a great player, I would have said a magician."

It took 10 years of hard work and a lot of growing up before Pat became a real star in basketball.

A few years ago while playing for the Georgetown Hoyas, Pat had real problems on the court. Whenever he was frustrated, he lost his cool. Word spread quickly. Players from other teams did every trick to shake up the seven-foot freshman. Too often, they succeeded in making him angry. He ended up missing key shots and throwing the ball away.

But before the season was over, Pat pulled himself together and learned to control his temper. As a result, he brought Georgetown College to the NCAA finals for the first time in the school's history. In his third year, he led the Georgetown Hoyas to the national championship. He became 1984's college basketball sensation. Today he is a top player for the New York Knicks.

His mother had a lot to do with his growing up in the right direction. Dorothy Ewing gave up an easy life in Jamaica to bring her son to Cambridge, Massachusetts and give him the best possible chance in life. She worked full time in a kitchen to keep her son in school. Before she died at 55, when Pat was a junior in college, Pat promised her he would graduate from Georgetown. That same year, the pros offered him millions of dollars to leave college and join the NBA. Everyone thought he would jump at the chance. So did John

Thompson, Pat's Georgetown coach whom Pat respects most. But Pat turned down the offer to keep his promise to his mother.

Pat graduated from Georgetown in June 1985 with a degree in fine arts. When reporters asked him what he thought his biggest accomplishment was—winning the 1983 NCAA championship for Georgetown or leading the U.S. team to a gold-medal victory in the 1984 Olympics?—Pat shook his head. He said he felt best about graduating and making true his mother's wish.

Check the best answer for each question.

1. Patrick Ewing really started to mature in basketball after he __.
   a. left Jamaica and joined the Georgetown Hoyas
   b. pulled himself together and learned to control his temper
   c. became a high school basketball star
   d. graduated from Georgetown College

2. When did Patrick Ewing "pull himself together" on the court?
   a. after he joined the New York Knicks
   b. during his high school days
   c. after his mother died
   d. before the end of his freshman year at Georgetown College

3. His mother brought him from Jamaica to Massachusetts to __.
   a. keep him away from trouble
   b. make him a basketball star
   c. give him the best chance in life
   d. make sure he earned a lot of money

4. Which of the following accomplishments did Patrick Ewing consider his best?
   a. He led the U.S. team to victory at the 1984 Olympics.
   b. He helped the Georgetown Hoyas become the 1983 NCAA champions.
   c. He earned more money as a professional player.
   d. He graduated from Georgetown College with a degree in fine arts.

5. Who influenced Patrick Ewing to finish college?
   a. his teachers   c. his high school coach
   b. his mother   d. his father

Guess Who's Joined the Team?

It was just a school football game. But everybody was there, including the media. TV and newspaper reporters were all over the place. Why all the excitement? The answer came when player number 18 took off her helmet. Elizabeth Balsley, age 16, was playing her first game with North Hunterdon's junior varsity football team in New Jersey.

"It's a great sport," she told reporters. She explained that people paid more attention to football than to any other sport.

To get in shape, she had to ride her bike 20 miles a day. But she had to do more than just getting in shape to get a slot in the team. She had to go to court to fight for her right to play. Most schools do not allow boys and girls to play together in contact sports like football. The court ruled in her favor. But she still had to win support from her teammates and classmates.

"Eighty per cent of the players don't want her on the team," said one of the boys.

Some coaches and girls who played all-female sports also objected to her joining the team. They said Elizabeth took away attention from the great female athletes in other sports. A girl in Elizabeth's school described her as an untalented player. "If she were a boy who couldn't play well enough, nobody would have wanted her on the team," the girl added.

Elizabeth, however, said she thought it only fair that girls have a chance to play football. She admitted she was the worst player on the team, but quickly explained that the boys had had more years at the game. "I'll give it everything I have to catch up," she promised.

That spirit won Elizabeth the support of many people. Geraldine Ferraro, the first woman to run for the U.S. vice-presidency, wrote Elizabeth: "I am rooting for you. You are a pioneer."

Choose the best answer for each question.

1. Elizabeth Balsley drew wide attention because she ___.
   a. was a good football player
   b. won a sports award
   c. scored the winning goal
   d. had to go to court to be allowed to join an all-male football team

2. The article emphasizes that ___.
   a. football should only be played by males
   b. members of football teams should be of the same sex
   c. there should be no sex discrimination in sports
   d. courts should intervene in sports controversies

3. Elizabeth's entry into the all-male football team was ___.
   a. welcomed by the players on the team
   b. objected to by some of the players
   c. objected to by the majority of the players
   d. welcomed by the coaches and other female athletes

4. According to Elizabeth, the boys were better players because ___.
   a. girls are the weaker sex
   b. the boys had been playing the game for a longer time
   c. the boys were more physically fit
   d. most girls disliked football

5. Elizabeth received the support of many people because ___.
   a. she was very popular
   b. she was very intelligent
   c. she displayed a strong spirit
   d. the court upheld her right to play football

6. Why did Geraldine Ferraro call Elizabeth a pioneer?
   a. Because Elizabeth was tough.
   b. Because Elizabeth stayed in good shape for the game.
   c. Because Elizabeth got the attention of the media.
   d. Because Elizabeth was the first girl to fight for her right to play football with an all-male team.

Eye Wonder

Everyone's eyelids close and open rapidly, or blink, for any number of reasons. One reason is that the eyes are protecting themselves from something that is irritating them. Another reason is that they are protecting themselves from a bright light. A third reason is that they are trying to keep themselves free from dirt and dust.

Every time you blink your eyes, you are actually crying, or producing tears. These tears keep your eyes wet. So that when an irritating substance, such as a bit of dirt, gets into your eye, your eyelids close and the tears try to wash away the dirt. A person blinks his or her eyes about 25 times per minute.

Every person has a blind spot. A blind spot is the point where you may be facing a small object and not be able to see it. The reason everyone has a blind spot is that there is one point on the retina where the optic nerve leaves your eye. No pictures or images are received because the point is not sensitive to light.

Try this experiment to find out where your blind spot is. Mark each side of this page with a visible dot. Hold this page about 12 inches in front of you. Close your left eye and leave your right eye open. Look only at the dot on the left. Now move the book slowly toward your face, then move it slowly away from your face. As you move it away, at a certain point the dot at the right side disappears totally. It is at that point that the dot falls exactly on your blind spot.

Just as you are either right-handed or left-handed, so are you either right-eyed or left-eyed. That means one of your eyes is stronger, or more dominant, than the other. Here's another experiment you can do to find out which is your dominant eye. Hold a pencil vertically at arm's length in front of you and at eye level. With both your eyes open, line up the pencil with a shelf, picture, clock or something else on the wall. First close one eye, then the other. Did the pencil stay in the same place with one eye open? Did it seem to move to the side of the other eye? Whichever eye was open when the pencil lined up with your object on the wall is your stronger, or dominant, eye.

Choose the best answer for each question.

1. According to the article, why do you blink your eyes?
   a. to protect them from dirt and dust
   b. to protect them from a bright light
   c. to protect them from irritating substances
   d. all of the above

2. The passage explains that the tears caused by blinking actually try to __.
   a. show how sad you are
   b. wash away dirt or dust that gets into your eyes
   c. keep the eyes moving
   d. all of the above

3. A person is either right-eyed or left-eyed, depending on which eye is __.
   a. bigger   c. rounder
   b. clearer   d. stronger

4. A blind spot is that point on the retina which is __.
   a. defective   c. not sensitive to light
   b. sensitive to light d. fully developed

5. The main purpose of the article is to __.
   a. explain defects in the eye
   b. describe functions of the optic nerve
   c. make you conduct experiments
   d. make you appreciate how your eyes function

How to Use Your Eyes and Ears

Helen Keller became blind and deaf when she was one year and seven months old. To communicate she learned to read braille. She also learned signed language and to "hear"—reading lips by touching the mouth of the speaker. The following is an excerpt from her autobiography:

Sometimes I have thought we should live each day as if it were our last. Most of us, however, take life for granted.

The same casualness characterizes the use of all our senses. Only the deaf appreciates hearing. Only the blind realizes the blessings that lie in sight. It's the same old story of not being grateful for what we have until we lose it.

I have often thought it would be a blessing if each human being were stricken blind and deaf for a few days. Darkness would make him appreciate sight. Silence would teach him the joys of sound.

Now and then I have tested my seeing friends to discover what they see. Recently I was visited by a good friend. She had just returned from a walk in the woods. "What did you see?" I asked. "Nothing in particular," was her reply.

How is it possible to walk for an hour and see nothing worthy of note? I cannot see, but I find hundreds of things that interest me. I feel the delicate patterns of a leaf. I pass my hand lovingly about the smooth skin of a birch or the rough bark of pine. In spring I touch the branches of trees in search of a bud. I feel the velvety texture of a flower. Occasionally, I place my hand on a small tree and feel the happy quiver of a bird in song.

At times I long to see all these things. If I can get so much pleasure from mere touch, how much more beauty must be revealed by sight. Yet those who have eyes see little. The panorama of color and action which fills the world is taken for granted.

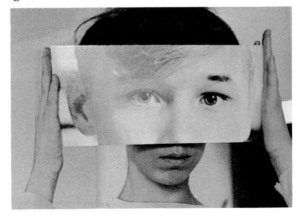

If I were the president of a university I would set up a course called "How to Use Your Eyes." The teacher would show his pupils how they could add joy to their lives by really seeing what passes unnoticed before them.

Choose the best answer for each question.

1. The selection is mainly about ___.
   a. how Helen Keller overcame her handicaps
   b. Helen Keller's thoughts about other people
   c. how Helen Keller became blind and deaf
   d. how people fail to really see and hear the beautiful things around them

2. What did Helen Keller suggest to make people appreciate fully the blessings of sight and hearing?
   a. Make them deaf and blind for a few days.
   b. Let people live their lives as if each day is the last day.
   c. Let schools set up a course on "How to Use Your Eyes."
   d. All of the above

3. How did Helen Keller "hear" what people said to her?
   a. She learned sign language.
   b. She touched their mouths as they spoke.
   c. She learned to read braille.
   d. She felt their pulse for vibrations.

4. Why did Helen Keller's friend say she saw nothing in particular after a walk in the woods?
   a. The woods were covered by snow.
   b. There were no flowers and birds in the woods.
   c. She probably took for granted what she usually saw in the woods.
   d. She was probably thinking of her children while walking in the woods.

5. How did Helen Keller "hear" a bird in song?
   a. by touching a tree and feeling it quiver while a bird sang
   b. by touching its beak
   c. by asking a friend to tell her through sign language
   d. by touching its feathers

LESSON 7

The Old Man and the "Giraffe"

They stood at the base of the high cliffs in Wisconsin—a young German and several young American climbers and an old man. The young German dared the Americans to climb the most dangerous cliff face—without a rope. This particular climb was called the "Giraffe." The overhang at the top of this climb was considered too dangerous to hurdle without a rope.

None of the young American climbers accepted the young German's challenge, but to his surprise the old man did. Now fifty years old, the brave man walked with a cane. He had a bad back and bad legs. Unknown to the young German, the brave man, Hawsmoot, used to be a great climber. He had never been thirty miles beyond his own town, but climbers from all over the world used to come and climb with him. But that was many years ago. Could he still do it?

The other climbers tried to talk him out of it. But Hawsmoot lay his cane carefully against the cliff and looked up at the massive cliff face which he had spent half his lifetime studying and climbing. Fear momentarily gripped him. Was he not too old to climb without a rope? But he set his fear aside and started climbing.

As he inched his way up the cliff, he thought about his early years. He remembered Meyers, who followed him up every cliff, except this one they named the "Giraffe." Even a world famous climber like Meyers dared not climb it because it was too dangerous.

When the old man reached the overhang, he stopped. He looked down and saw the young climbers below, craning their necks as they watched him. It was a long way down. If he misjudged the swing up onto the overhang, he would fall to his death. He grabbed hold of the rock and dangled there. He felt a great desire to let go. He felt exhausted. But he hung on. He pulled his head up to level with his hands. His muscles were so tight he thought they would burst through the skin. He kicked and swung one leg up. He missed the foothold. He hung out over the emptiness. His body screamed for him to let go. Many climbers had missed the foothold and fell, but they had ropes to stop them from falling to their deaths. The old man

74

held tight, then swung again. This time he made it. He pulled himself onto the overhang.

The young German waited for him at the top. They faced each other in the wind that blew over the cliffs.

"You are a great climber," the young German said and shook his hand.

The old man looked out over Wisconsin. He was not too old, after all.

Check the best answer for each question.

1. Which of the following states the main idea of the story?
   a. Old climbers easily get exhausted.
   b. Climbing without a rope is very dangerous.
   c. To prove his worth, a determined person challenges great odds.
   d. Young climbers are better than old ones.

2. Why was the cliff face called the "Giraffe?"
   a. Because giraffes fed on the grass below the cliff.
   b. Because it was a steep high climb with an overhang near the top.
   c. Because the cliff face had two holes resembling a giraffe's eyes.
   d. Somebody just named it the "Giraffe" for no reason at all.

3. Why did no one else accept the young German's challenge to climb the "Giraffe?"
   a. Because no one had climbed it before without a rope.
   b. They preferred climbing the other cliffs.
   c. They did not like the young German.
   d. They wanted the old man to do it.

4. Hawsmoot felt confident he could climb the "Giraffe" without a rope because ___.
   a. it was a cliff in his town
   b. he was the best climber in the world
   c. he spent half his life studying and climbing it
   d. he did not fear climbing any cliff

5. When Hawsmoot succeeded climbing the cliff without a rope, the young German ___.
   a. hated him
   b. admired him
   c. told him to stop climbing
   d. told him to keep on climbing

Practice your critical-reading skills in the following three selections. Read the test tips before you read each selection. Put your answers on your answer sheet.

Test Tips: An incorrect answer choice on a test is often partly true, but not entirely true. Be sure to choose the best answer of the four.

Everyone needs help remembering. Many people use mnemonics which are little tricks to jog the memory. The word comes from the Greek goddess of memory, Mnemosyne. She was the mother of the muses who were the goddesses of music, art, literature, and other arts.

Some mnemonics are acronyms. For example, HOMES is an acronym or a memory code made from the first letter in the name of each of the Great Lakes: Lake Huron, Lake Ontario, Lake Michigan, Lake Erie, and Lake Superior. "Every Good Boy Does Fine" is an acronym for the five lines of the music scale, E, G, B, D, and F

Some mnemonics are rhymes like "Thirty days hath September / April, June, and November; / February has twenty-eight until the time / Leap year gives it twenty-nine." Many people still use this mnemonic to remember how many days are in each month.

Most mnemonics are more simple. Politicians often make them up to help remember people's names. Students use them, too, to remember things like lists, dates, and facts for examinations. Try writing one yourself!

---

1. Mnemonics are good ___.
   a. goddesses   c. acronyms
   b. rhymes   d. memory aids

2. The main purpose of this article is ___.
   a. to discuss mnemonics
   b. to tell about the Greeks
   c. to encourage rhyming
   d. to help politicians

3. People have ___.
   a. developed mnemonics only recently
   b. not properly used their memory
   c. been using mnemonics for centuries
   d. seldom used memory aids

4. In the author's opinion, mnemonics are ___.
   a. overrated   c. for children
   b. useful   d. a waste of time

There is a program that tries to make math and science fun for elementary and high school students. The program uses toys, sports, and games to teach such things as the principles of physics and math.

The program, called the Young Astronaut Program, really has nothing to do with training young people to become astronauts. It is the brain child of well-known journalist Jack Anderson. He founded the program when he realized that our country is being left behind in the industrial revolution. Our technology, he explained, can only keep pace with that of the rest of the world if we train more young people in the fields of math and science. But he found out only 6% of American students graduate with skills in math, science and technology. The Soviet Union, Japan and West Germany are graduating 70% to 90% of their students proficient in these areas.

The program, launched in 1985, has been getting a good response among the youth. In the first four months, about 25,000 students (51% girls and 49% boys) signed up for the program.

The goal of the Young Astronaut Program is to help students realize that whatever they become, they will be living in an age of lasers, computers, robots and other hi-tech tools of the modern age.

5. The main purpose of the article is to ___.
   a. encourage student participation in the program
   b. change student curricula
   c. make America number one in technology
   d. explain training of astronauts

6. The program attracts student participants by making the study of math and science ___.
   a. difficult   c. fun
   b. unimportant   d. useful

7. What percent of American students graduate with math and science skills?
   a. 25%   c. 50%
   b. 8%   d. 6%

8. The students' response to the program has been ___.
   a. disappointing c. enthusiastic
   b. minimal   d. negative

9. The writer's attitude toward the program appears to be ___.
   a. enthusiastic   c. confused
   b. disappointed d. alarmed

Test Tips: When reading a poem, look for opinions and feelings that the poet is expressing. Questions on a test are likely to ask about a poet's opinions and feelings.

Hold fast to dreams
For if dreams die
Life is a broken-winged bird
That cannot fly.

Hold fast to dreams
For when dreams go
Life is a barren field
Frozen with snow.

Langston Hughes

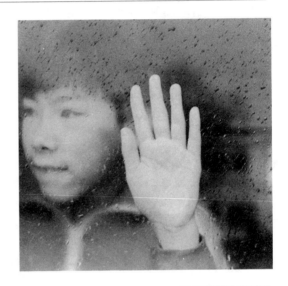

10. The poet's mood in this poem is ___.
    a. angry
    b. desperate
    c. pleased
    d. disappointed

11. The words *broken-winged* in the third line suggest that ___.
    a. life can't exist without dreams
    b. life without dreams is frustrating
    c. life is satisfactory
    d. dreams can be tiresome

12. Which of these is the best title for the poem?
    a. "A Sad Poet"
    b. "An Empty Life"
    c. "Birds and Snow"
    d. "Dreams"

13. The poet feels that a life without dreams ___.
    a. is one in which nothing wonderful can happen
    b. creates an ugly environment
    c. makes people cold and uncaring
    d. can be as productive as life with dreams

UNIT II
VOCABULARY

PART 1

Synonyms and Antonyms

You often have to explain the meaning of a new word you come across in your reading or on a vocabulary test. In Part 1, you are going to practice two methods of understanding and explaining the meaning of an unfamiliar word. First, you will learn to define a new word by matching it with a word or phrase that has almost the same meaning. Next, you will learn to define a new word by matching it with a word or phrase that has the opposite meaning. Your matches will help you understand and correctly use the new words you will meet in the reading selections and activities in Part 1.

Look for matches in the car ads below. Try to find two car ads that have almost the same meaning. Also, match two ads that have opposite meanings. Write your matches on your paper.

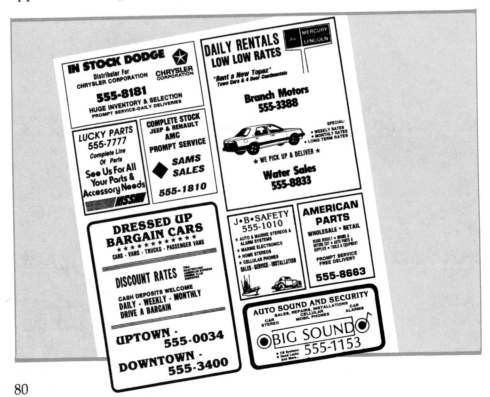

SYNONYMS AND MEANING

Two words that have almost the same meaning are called *synonyms*. The simplest way to explain the meaning of a new word is to use its synonym as a definition. For example, *circuitous* and *indirect* are synonyms. One way to define *circuitous* is to say it means "indirect."

Some questions on vocabulary tests ask for the best synonym for a difficult word. Each synonym has its own shade of meaning. Usually one synonym fits better in one sentence than another. For example, you might take a *circuitous* way around a city to avoid traffic; you might be *indirectly* involved in an accident if you drive at a speed of 15 miles an hour in a 55 mph-maximum speed limit zone.

Read the paragraph below about the popular subject of stress. Three difficult words in the paragraph are printed in dark type.

Stress is a word we hear frequently these days. It means a **constraining** factor that puts pressure on us. We all have problems and pressures. No one is **exempt**. But some seem to suffer more than others. Some people get high blood pressure or ulcers or rashes or pains. Even the common cold is now considered stress-related. But there are other people who seem to **thrive** on stress. Why? Medical research indicates that people with "hardy" personalities build up for themselves a strong immune system that inoculates the body against stress-related illnesses.

Which word in dark type is a synonym of *restricting*? Which is a synonym of *free*? Which is a synonym of *grow* or *prosper*?

Reread the paragraph. Substitute *restricting* for **constraining**, *free* for **exempt**, and *grow* for **thrive**. Did using the synonyms help you understand the paragraph more easily?

Do the activities on the next two pages to learn more about using synonyms to explain the meanings of new words.

A. Look at the words in List 1 below. They were all used in the paragraph about stress. You will find a synonym for each word in List 2. Write the matches on your paper.

LIST 1
1. frequently
2. factor
3. problems
4. researchers
5. inoculates

LIST 2
a. element
b. immunizes
c. often
d. troubles
e. investigators

Check your answers. Reread the paragraph on stress. Substitute the words in List 2 for their synonyms in List 1. If the paragraph makes sense, your answers are right.

B. Read the next paragraph which tells you what the characteristics of the "hardy" personality are. Notice the words in dark type.

The immune system apparently responds to what is in the mind. Researchers say that even if a person is not a "hardy" type, he can pretend he is and fool his own immune system. He must **alter** his thinking and his vocabulary. Instead of becoming **apprehensive** at the idea of change, he can view change as a chance for a new beginning. Instead of being weighed down by **obligations** to people, he can think of **commitments** to people. Instead of **anticipating** the results of good luck or bad luck, he can think of himself as a person who takes the **initiative**, and thus controls a situation.

Decide which word in dark type in the paragraph is the correct answer for each question below. Put your answers on your paper.

1. Which word is a synonym of *anxious*?
2. Which word is a synonym of *change*?
3. Which word is a synonym of *expecting*?
4. Which word is a synonym of *duties*?
5. Which word is a synonym of *promises*?
6. Which word is a synonym of *active role*?

Check your answers. Reread the paragraph. Substitute the synonyms from the questions for the words in dark type. If the paragraph still makes sense to you, your answers are right.

C. Here are the kinds of questions you often see on vocabulary tests. Look at the word in dark type at the top of each item. Then pick the answer that means the same, or almost the same, as the word in dark type. Put your answers on your paper.

---

1. a **constraining** influence
   a. good
   b. restricting
   c. harmful

2. a **thriving** business
   a. growing
   b. slow
   c. failing

3. tax **exempt**
   a. included
   b. excused
   c. deducted

4. dress **alterations**
   a. changes
   b. prices
   c. sizes

5. **anticipating** a raise
   a. proposing
   b. demanding
   c. expecting

6. on his **initiative**
   a. own effort
   b. self-interest
   c. instruction

Check your answers: You should have picked **b** for 1, **a** for 2, **b** for 3, **a** for 4, **c** for 5, and **a** for 6. If you didn't get those answers, reread pages 81–82.

LESSON 1

Here are the eight new words in this lesson. Next to each word is a word or phrase that has almost the same meaning. Look for the new words in the passage below. Use the synonyms to help you understand the lesson words.

resin—gum or sap
masticate—chew
viscous—non-flowing
entrepreneur—originator

initiated—introduced or began
pragmatic—useful or practical
enhanced—improved
attest—prove

The Ancient Chewing Gum

For thousands of years, people have been chewing gum. The ancient Greeks chewed the **resin** of the mastic tree. Their word "mastike" which meant "to chew" is almost the same as our word **masticate**. Today, the **viscous** liquid of the little evergreen mastic tree is used not for gum, but to make glue or mastic for such things as laying tile.

Our chewing gum is made from the resin of the Sapodilla tree grown in Mexico and Central America. The Mayan Indians discovered, made and used the gum which they then called "chicle." We sometimes still call today's chewing gum *chiclet*.

Lumps of gum were chewed in North America around the time of the Civil War. But it took a young American **entrepreneur** at the turn of the century to come up with the product so popular in America today.

William Wrigley **initiated** a very **pragmatic** approach to the production of chewing gum. First, he realized that a few drops of peppermint or spearmint oil combined with sweeteners greatly **enhanced** the flavor. Later he learned to double the flavor, hence—double the fun, and double his profits. He developed a machine for packaging slices of gum individually in wax paper and aluminum foil. By 1913, he was into advertising and clever sales promotions that made the retail stores happy to carry his gum. Soon chewing gum was everywhere—not only in mouths, but on the soles of shoes, under desks, and stuck to the carpet. Wrigley became a rich man, as the Wrigley Building in Chicago and Wrigley estate on Catalina Island off Los Angeles **attest**.

A. Decide which one of the lesson words should be used to fill the blank in each sentence below. Use the synonyms on page 84 to help you choose the right answers. Also notice the way the new words were used in the passage. Write your answers on your paper.

1. Steven Jobs is an American __ who started the Apple Computer Corporation.
2. Glue and varnish are some of the products made from __.
3. It is difficult to __ when you are wearing braces on your teeth.
4. Herbs and spices have always __ the flavor of food.
5. The current low incidence of dental cavities among children can __ to the fact that knowledge of dental hygiene has improved.
6. Diesel fuel and heavy oils tend to become __ in very cold weather.
7. Senator Dosomething __ a program of tax reform.
8. You may not enjoy this class, but since you need it to graduate, be __ and pass it!

B. Look at the word in dark type in each item below. Decide which answer is a synonym of the word in dark type. Put your answers on your paper.

1. **attest** to the fact
   a. true
   b. attach
   c. testify

2. **enhanced** the appearance
   a. improved
   b. spoiled
   c. changed

3. **initiate** a program
   a. improve
   b. introduce
   c. prevent

4. a **pragmatic** person
   a. kind
   b. attractive
   c. practical

C. Write a sentence to answer each question below. Use the word in dark type in your answer.

1. Who was the **entrepreneur** who introduced the Model T Ford?
2. Do nuts **enhance** the flavor of chocolate chip cookies?
3. Do snakes **masticate**?

LESSON 2

Here are the eight new words in this lesson. Next to each word is a word or phrase that has almost the same meaning. Look for the new words in the passage below. Use the synonyms to help you understand the lesson words.

revolutionize—change
destitute—very poor
diversification—variation
by-products—additional things or outgrowths

foundation—organization
unassuming—modest or humble
acclaimed—praised
fellow—comrade or associate

Much More Than Peanuts

George Washington Carver was born a slave on a farm near Diamond Grove, Missouri. When he was a child, the Emancipation Proclamation freed him from slavery. He showed great ability in school, especially in painting and in biology. Because he loved plants, he chose to become a scientist and help **revolutionize** the lives of the poor southern farmers.

He earned his way through school and graduated from Iowa State College of Agriculture and Mechanical Arts. He was a member of the faculty there until, at the invitation of Booker T. Washington, another great black leader, he joined the staff of Tuskegee Institute in Alabama where he remained for the rest of his life.

Cotton had been the crop of the south but cotton farmers then were becoming **destitute**. Carver taught them crop **diversification**. He showed them they could grow peanuts, pecans, and sweet potatoes on their land. But the farmers could not sell their products. So Carver experimented in his laboratory. He developed over 300 **by-products** from peanuts alone. Peanut butter is the best known, but he also made dyes, plastics, milk powder, flour, and wood stain. From the sweet potato, he made flour, shoe polish, and candy. From wood shavings, he made synthetic marble and fiber boards.

Carver also used all his savings to establish a **foundation** for agricultural research. On the farm where he was born, is the George Washington Carver National Monument. It stands as a tribute to this quiet, **unassuming** agricultural chemist. He had also been **acclaimed** internationally as an artist and was elected a **fellow** of the Royal Society of Arts in London, an honor few Americans have received.

A. Decide which one of the lesson words should be used to fill the blank in each sentence below. Use the synonyms in the lesson to help you choose the right answers. Also notice the way the new words were used in the passage. Write your answers on your paper.

1. He was a ___ soldier and comrade of mine in the army.
2. She left her money to a ___ for the care of homeless parakeets.
3. Large corporations interested in ___ may own several businesses.
4. Successful space shuttle launches will eventually ___ travel.
5. The chief was an ___ man who never boasted about himself.
6. The terrible drought in the West has left many farmers ___.
7. Bark and wood chip businesses are really ___ of the lumber industry.
8. Bruce Springsteen was widely ___ for helping American workmen.

B. Look at the word in dark type in each item below. Decide which answer is a synonym of the word in dark type. Put your answers on your paper.

1. **unassuming** attitude
   a. silly
   b. frightened
   c. modest

2. charitable **foundation**
   a. idea
   b. organization
   c. place

3. **revolutionize** the system
   a. change
   b. destroy
   c. establish

4. a **destitute** woman
   a. very rich
   b. very pretty
   c. very poor

C. Write a sentence to answer each question below. Use the lesson word in dark type in your sentence.

1. Who is the most highly **acclaimed** movie star today?
2. Name one **by-product** of peanuts.
3. What does crop **diversification** mean?

87

LESSON 3

Here are the eight new words in this lesson. Next to each word is a word or phrase that has almost the same meaning. Look for the new words in the passage below. Use the synonyms to help you understand the lesson words.

phenomenon—strange happening or occurrence
manifest—evident or seen
advantageous—fortunate or favorable
hues—colors

prevalent—common
collide—clash or crash together
celestial—heavenly or in the sky
profoundly—deeply

The Aurora Borealis

Ever since man has been on Earth looking up at the sky, he has been filled with wonder at the beauty of what he has seen. One of these sights is the *Aurora Borealis*. This is a beautiful, natural **phenomenon** of arcs and streaks of light that flow across the sky in early spring and fall. The name means "northern dawn." There is also an *Aurora Australis* or "southern dawn." Ancient man believed it was Aurora, the dawn goddess, who helped open the gates of Heaven each morning so that the sun god, Apollo, could ride out in his chariot and bring the sun's light to the world.

Although the Aurora Borealis is **manifest** mostly in the northern part of the Northern Hemisphere, it can also be seen in the United States and as far south as Mexico when atmospheric conditions are **advantageous**. Its long beams of flickering light seem constantly to change **hues** as they wave across the sky. The most **prevalent** hue is green, though some are also red, blue, and violet. The green is caused by atomic oxygen and the red by nitrogen and molecular oxygen. These differences in color are caused by different gases.

The displays are electrical and have some connection with magnetic storms. They are caused when protons and electrons are shot from the sun into the Earth's upper atmosphere. The poles act as magnets to attract the particles. As the particles move, they **collide** with Earth's atmospheric particles and change their electrical charge. This causes them to glow like the charged particles in a fluorescent light tube.

In spite of all the knowledge we have today about what is happening in the **celestial** atmosphere, we are still **profoundly** awed by the beauty of it all, just as were the ancient Greeks and Romans who thought a goddess was up there controlling the dawn light. Our knowledge of things may change, but our sense of wonder remains a driving force of life.

A. Decide which one of the lesson words should be used to fill the blank in each sentence below. Use the synonyms on page 88 to help you choose the right answers. Also notice the way the new words were used in the passage. Write your answers on your paper.

1. The varied ___ of the flags waving in the wind gave the racetrack a festive appearance.
2. It would be ___ for anyone to know how to use a computer.
3. The habit of smoking is less ___ in our school than it was a year ago.
4. The appearance of a ghost is a strange ___ no one could explain.
5. The old name of China was the ___ Empire, probably because the rulers considered it heavenly, supreme, and close to the sky.
6. Henry's good education was ___ in his work and his manners.
7. She was ___ moved by his pleas for forgiveness.
8. When two different personalities ___, problems are bound to arise.

B. Read each incomplete sentence below. Decide which answer best completes the sentence. Put your answers on your paper.

1. An unusual phenomenon is a ___.
   a. haunted building
   b. strange occurrence
   c. strange person

2. A prevalent custom is often ___.
   a. avoided
   b. doubted
   c. followed

3. If your dress is a brilliant hue, it is ___.
   a. black
   b. colorful
   c. white

4. An advantageous situation is ___.
   a. good
   b. unfortunate
   c. new

C. Write a sentence to answer each question below. Use the lesson word in dark type in your sentence.

1. Do you know the names of any of the **celestial** constellations?
2. What precaution must racing cyclists take in case they **collide**?
3. List two events that you feel were **advantageous** for you.

LESSON 4

Here are the eight new words in this lesson. Next to each word is a word or phrase that has almost the same meaning. Look for the new words in the passage below. Use the synonyms to help you understand the lesson words.

surmised—guessed
legend—unverified story
loner—unsociable person
cultivated—grown

disseminated—spread
devastated—ruined
domesticated—tamed
unverified—unproven

An Ancient Fruit

Many of us grew up with the vague idea that without a hero named Johnny Appleseed, there would be no apples in our lunch boxes today. Somehow, we **surmised** he was the one who found out how good apples were at keeping the doctor away. All that is merely a **legend**. Actually, Johnny was the American pioneer, John Chapman, born in Massachusetts. He moved and farmed first in western Pennsylvania and then in Ohio. He did distribute apple seeds to some people in Ohio, Indiana, and Illinois. Otherwise he was pretty much of a **loner**. After an article called "Johnny Appleseed, a Pioneer Hero" was written in Harper's *New Monthly Magazine* in 1871, the folktales and legends began. And they have been told and retold for over 100 years!

Apples have been a source of food as far back as ancient civilization goes. Archeologists have found burnt apples in their diggings. The Greeks **cultivated** several varieties as early as 300 B.C. The Romans **disseminated** the knowledge of apple cultivation all over Europe. Then when Roman civilization was **devastated** by the barbarians, the monks of the Middle Ages saved the knowledge of growing fruits and taught the barbarians about the "malus domestica" (the scientific name for the **domesticated** species of apples), along with Christianity.

The apple, which is a member of the rose family, was especially popular in England. From there the early colonists brought it to America. And here it flourishes today, as American as apple pie and as sweet as apple cider. Although its use as preventative medicine still remains **unverified**, the apple lover keeps eating one apple a day to keep the doctor away.

A. Decide which one of the lesson words should be used to fill the blank in each sentence below. Use the synonyms on page 90 to help you choose the right answers. Also notice the way the new words were used in the passage. Write your answers on your paper.

1. A newspaper __ information about the secret arms deal.
2. An entire city can be __ by a bomb attack.
3. We __ peaches as well as apples on our farm.
4. I __ from your attitude that you had a terrible time.
5. Every school has someone who is a __, doing and minding his own business.
6. A judge cannot accept information that is __.
7. After she __ the skunk, her family made her put it back in the woods.
8. Once he scored the winning goal, he became a __ in his own mind.

B. Read each incomplete sentence below. Decide which answer best completes the sentence. Put your answers on your paper.

1. A legend is a story that has __.
   a. some element of truth
   b. no truth
   c. all truth

2. A loner is a person who __.
   a. loves parties
   b. hates people
   c. likes to be alone

3. When you surmised something you were __.
   a. lying about it
   b. not sure of it
   c. proving it

4. If a person feels devastated, he feels __.
   a. terribly upset
   b. happy
   c. surprised

C. Write a sentence to answer each question below. Use the lesson word in dark type in your sentence.

1. What are four **domesticated** animals?
2. What is your favorite **legend**?
3. How would you **disseminate** information about a new product?

LESSON 5

Here are the 10 new words in this lesson. Next to each word is a word or phrase that has almost the same meaning. Look for the new words in the passage below. Use the synonyms to help you understand the lesson words.

menace—threat
obnoxious—hateful
monopolizing—dominating
bravado—pretended courage
competent—capable or skilled

heed—follow
deprecating—disapproving
blemish—defect or imperfection
feedback—reaction
reiterates—repeats

Be Your Own Fan!

If you have already passed your driving test, you know that self-confidence is important to a driver. A driver with little self-confidence hesitates at the wrong times and could be a real **menace** on the road. A driver with too much self-confidence is a fool who risks his own neck as well as everybody else's. Just the right amount of confidence is needed in other areas, too. A student in the classroom with too little self-confidence has difficulty participating. Whereas, an over-confident student can be **obnoxious**, talking too much and **monopolizing** the discussions.

The foolish driver and the obnoxious student do not demonstrate self-confidence. What they reveal is a need to hide their lack of it under a show of **bravado**. If a person is truly confident, there is no need for showing off.

The first step in building up confidence is action. In driving, you become a competent driver by practice. You have to drive in bad weather, in heavy traffic, and on busy highways. As you become more **competent** you acquire more confidence. It is the same with building confidence in yourself as a student. The more you participate in a class discussion, speak in front of the class, assume other responsibilities— the more you hear a tiny voice inside saying, "Well done. Keep it up." The trick is to **heed** that voice when facing difficult situations.

It is hard to be confident when people say **deprecating** things to us. You arrive in a new outfit and someone says "Wow!" That helps. But if someone says, "You look terrific. That ugly **blemish** on your nose hardly shows at all!"—that doesn't help much. The point is, do not rely on **feedback** from others to build your confidence. Decide for yourself what you are like, what you can do, and let the praise or criticism flutter past you. Listen instead to that voice inside which **reiterates**, "Well done." Listen to it. Then believe it.

A. Decide which one of the lesson words should be used to fill the blank in each sentence below. Use the synonyms from the lesson to help you choose the right answers. Also notice the way the new words were used in the aritcle. Write your answers on your paper.

1. If you __ your driving instructor's advice, you'll get your driver's license.
2. We have had no __ from the public about how they like our show.
3. Anyone who insists on __ the conversation is a bore.
4. Tornadoes are a real __ in Kansas and the flat parts of Ohio.
5. Throwing food in the cafeteria is __ behavior.
6. Jim is a __ craftsman; look at the beautiful chair he made.
7. Assuming an air of __, the dog barked furiously at the motorcycle.
8. I will not listen to __ remarks about my good friend Dennis.
9. The reddish birthmark on her chin is the only __ on her face.
10. Our teacher __ everything until he is hoarse.

B. Look at each sentence below. Decide which answer is the best synonym for the word in italics in the sentence. Put your answers on your paper.

1. With great *bravado,* the circus clown walked a tightrope one foot above the ground.
   a. courage
   b. humor
   c. pretended courage

2. The town thought that the new plant would be a *menace* because of the pollution it would cause.
   a. help
   b. threat
   c. improvement

3. His public record was perfect, without any *blemish,* until he was linked to the scandal.
   a. defect
   b. distinction
   c. interruption

4. If we *heed* the teacher's advice, we will do well on the exam.
   a. like
   b. follow
   c. disregard

C. Write a sentence to answer each question below. Use the lesson word in dark type in your answer.

1. Who is the most **competent** cook you know?
2. Do people who make **deprecating** remarks become popular?
3. What word does your teacher **reiterate** most often?

Here are 10 facts you have learned in Lessons 1–5. The words written in italics are synonyms of the 10 lesson words listed below the fact sentences. Rewrite the sentences, using the lesson words to replace their synonyms.

1. Resin from an evergreen tree is a *non-flowing* substance that we call sap.

2. Wrigley was the man who *introduced* the process of packaging chewing gum in America and made a fortune on it.

3. George Washington Carver was a brilliant black man who *drastically changed* farming methods in the South.

4. He is *honored* by all Americans for his contributions to agricultural science.

5. In the spring, the Aurora Borealis is *evident* in the northern sky.

6. It is made up of many *colors*, especially green.

7. The *unproven stories* about Johnny Appleseed are based on some facts from the life of John Chapman.

8. The ancient Greeks and Romans *grew* several varieties of apples.

9. It takes effort and practice to become a *skilled* mechanic.

10. The *pretended courage* of show-offs is a cover-up for their lack of confidence.

LESSON WORDS

bravado	viscous
cultivated	revolutionized
hues	manifest
acclaimed	legends
initiated	competent

ANTONYMS AND MEANING

Some words mean just the opposite of each other. Two words that have opposite meanings are called *antonyms*. You can often use the antonym to help you understand and define an unfamiliar word. You can say that the new word means the opposite of its antonym.

For example, the words *fastidious* and *messy* are antonyms. You know what *messy* means. You can figure out that *fastidious* must mean "very neat and tidy."

Sometimes you can change a word into its opposite by adding a prefix such as *ab, in, non,* or *dis*. What do you think is the meaning of these words: *abnormal, indiscreet, nonresident,* and *disinclined*?

Three words are printed in dark type in the following explanation of a common expression. Use antonyms to help explain their meanings.

Consider the word "leftist" or "leftwing" which is used to describe a political **radical**. The word "left" has always had a **negative** feeling or connotation. The Latin word for "left" means sinister or evil. The French word for "left" means awkward or *gauche*. Whether it is intentional or not, most European legislatures seat their conservative members to the right of the chairman and their radical members to the left. At a **formal** dinner, the important guests are seated at the host's right. This indicates special respect for them. In the British Parliament, the members who were to get the most respect because they were in agreement with the chairman were known as parties of "the right wing." Those who were in the opposition became known as the radicals or parties of the "left wing" or "leftists."

Here are the three words and their antonyms. The words mean the opposite of their antonyms. Write the correct meanings on your paper.

radical—conservative
negative—positive
formal—casual

A. Read the following passage. Notice the words in dark type.

The American language is full of foreign expressions. Consider the word that is often said when a person sneezes. "Gesundheit!" This German word, which means "health," is also said during a cocktail drink *toast* to honor someone, or as a **blessing**—with wishes for good health and prosperity.

The word "cocktail" has several possible **origins**. Some say it was derived from an ancient Aztec drink offered to the Indian emperor, Xochiti. Some say it is from a blend of bitters and spirits fed to fighting cocks, to **induce** a state of violent movement or **agitation**, thus a "cocktail." As for that **tidbit** of food served with cocktails, we have the French word "hors d'oeuvre," meaning "outside the work." The chefs used the word to mean *food before the main dinner.*

Decide which word in dark type in the passage is the best one to complete each sentence below. Put your answers on your paper.

1. *Prevent* is the opposite of __.   **4.** *Bunch* is the opposite of __.
2. *Calmness* is the opposite of __.   **5.** *Endings* is the opposite of __.
3. *Curse* is the opposite of __.

Check your answers. Clues in the passage help you decide the answers are: 1. induce, 2. agitation, 3. blessing, 4. tidbit, 5. origins.

B. Read each vocabulary test item below. Choose the answer that means the opposite of the word in dark type. Make sure you choose an antonym and not a synonym. Put your answers on your paper.

1. a **radical** person
   a. rebellious
   b. conservative
   c. excitable

2. **abnormal** reaction
   a. common
   b. unusual
   c. interesting

3. in a state of **agitation**
   a. annoyance
   b. nervousness
   c. calmness

4. a **tidbit** of gossip
   a. great deal
   b. little amount
   c. word or two

Check your answers. Did you pick **b** for 1, **a** for 2, **c** for 3, and **a** for 4?

LESSON 6

Here are the eight new words in this lesson. Next to each word is a word or phrase that has almost the same meaning. Look for the new words in the passage below. Use the synonyms to help you understand the lesson words.

incontestable—proven
configuration—pattern
alleged—so-called
tampered—meddled

disavowal—denial
redress—correct or make right
cognizant—knowledgeable
unique—one of a kind

Incontestable Evidence

Each one of us is an original. **Incontestable** evidence of this is in our fingerprints. Every person has ten fingers and a fine skin pattern on the tip of each, yet no two people have exactly the same **configuration**. Consider these cases. A lost child is found after 5 years. An employee is **alleged** to have **tampered** with a safe. What is the indisputable evidence that proves who the child is? What is the positive proof that beats the employee's **disavowal** or which will **redress** the insult? Fingerprints. They are being used to make positive identification of people by the armed forces, by the government, by companies, and more recently by parents.

A person's fingerprints are formed before birth. They are clearly identifiable after a baby is 6 weeks old, and never change. People have been **cognizant** of this for centuries. The ancient Chinese used thumb prints as signatures as far back as 2,500 years. But not until the 1800's did modern people put to any practical use—the knowledge that each person's fingerprints are **unique**. Then an Englishman, Sir Francis Galton, dedicated his life to classifying fingerprints and organizing information for use in capturing criminals.

Although each person's prints are different, they fall into one of four general patterns. The arch has lines going from side to side in a more or less straight line pattern. The loop has lines curving back in a horseshoe pattern. The print with lines in a circular pattern is called the *whorl*. The print with a mixture of all these is called the *composite*.

While fingerprints have been treated in the past only as a means of identifying criminals, they are far more than that. They are a marvelous and simple proof that each one of us is a unique individual.

A. Each word or phrase below means the opposite of one of the new words in this lesson. On your paper, write down the lesson word that is the antonym of each word listed. For help, reread the synonyms listed beside the lesson words on page 98. Also notice how the new words were used in the passage.

1. common
2. unproven
3. ignorant
4. admission

5. random formation
6. injure or do wrong to
7. certain
8. left untouched

B. Choose a word that means the opposite of the word in dark type in each item below. Make sure you pick an antonym. Put your answers on your paper.

1. a **unique** painting
   a. unusual
   b. common
   c. only one of its kind

2. the **alleged** criminal
   a. proven
   b. accused
   c. so-called

3. to **redress** a wrong
   a. right
   b. prove
   c. cause

4. strange **configuration** of numbers
   a. mixture
   b. sum
   c. pattern

C. Write a sentence to answer each question below. Use the lesson word in dark type in your sentence.

1. In what subject are you most **cognizant**—cars, clothes, TV, or cooking?
2. Why are fingerprints **incontestable** proof of a person's identity?
3. Could you tell if someone has been **tampering** with your car or bike?

LESSON 7

Here are the eight new words in this lesson. Next to each new word is a word or phrase that has almost the same meaning. Look for the new words in the story below. Use the synonyms to help you understand the lesson words.

ingenious—clever
intricate—complicated
feigned—pretended
significant—important

gullible—believing (anything)
malevolent—evil
dissembling—disguising
enchanting—fascinating

The Ingenious Princess

Sheherazade was a beautiful, talented young princess in an ancient Arabian kingdom. As was the custom in those days, she was sent off to be married to a wealthy ruler called the Caliph. This Caliph, Shahriyar, was not an admirable fellow. He liked marrying beautiful girls. So, every night he would put his latest bride to death and marry another one the next day. But Sheherazade was an **ingenious** girl. On their wedding night, she began to tell an exciting and **intricate** tale. When she came to the most tense moment in the story, she **feigned** exhaustion and said she would finish the story the next night. On the

following evening, she did finish the story but started another. Then she would stop again at a **significant** moment. The Caliph was as **gullible** as he was **malevolent** because he fell for all this **dissembling**. She kept it up for 1,001 nights. At the end of that time, the Caliph was so much in love with her and found her so **enchanting** that he wanted no other wife.

This is how the collection of short stories known as *The Arabian Nights* or *Thousand and One Nights* was supposed to have come about. The collection includes "Sinbad the Sailor,"

"Ali Baba and the Forty Thieves," and "Alladin and His Wonderful Lamp." You may not have read these stories, but you probably have seen them in some version of Saturday morning TV cartoons. They were folk tales from India, Persia, Egypt, and Arabia, compiled about 500 years ago. Whether the story of Sheherazade is true or just another folktale, we will never know, but it is as interesting as any of the stories she is said to have told old Shahriyar.

A. Each word below means the opposite of one of the new words in this lesson. On your paper, write the lesson word that is the antonym of each word listed. For help, reread the synonyms listed beside the lesson words on page 100. Notice how the lesson words were used in the story.

1. uninteresting
2. stupid
3. simple
4. good
5. least important
6. skeptical
7. acted honestly
8. acting naturally

B. Read each incomplete sentence below. Decide which answer best completes the sentence. Put your answers on your paper.

1. If you feigned illness, you were not __.
   a. very ill
   b. well
   c. getting ill

2. An ingenious plan is not __.
   a. careless
   b. clever
   c. stupid

3. An intricate design is not __.
   a. simple
   b. complicated
   c. copied

4. Something significant is not __.
   a. important
   b. worthless
   c. surprising

C. Write a sentence to answer each question below. Use the lesson word in dark type in your sentence.

1. Who is the most **enchanting** person you have ever met?
2. What **malevolent** character of a person do "you love to hate?"
3. What would make you suspect a person was pretty **gullible**?

Here are the 10 new words in this lesson. Next to each word is a word or phrase that has almost the same meaning. Look for the new words in the passage below. Use the synonyms to help you understand the lesson words.

renewal—restoration
debunk—expose as false
obliterated—erased or removed
hoopla—commotion
anonymity—being unknown

unobtrusive—unnoticeable
restitution—reparation or payment
psychic—spiritualistic
autonomous—self-governing
rehabilitation—reeducation

Heroes Anonymous

On March 1, 1941, when *The Saturday Evening Post* was only 5 cents, Jack Alexander wrote a story for the famous magazine about Alcoholics Anonymous and its message of spiritual **renewal**. He intended at first to **debunk** the group, but after investigating the organization and seeing all the lives it had changed and all the misery it had **obliterated**, he had only praise for it. His story reached thousands of people who needed to read it. The group grew, and by July of 1985 when the organization was celebrating its 50th birthday, there were over a million members. The birthday was observed without any **hoopla** because such loud celebration is contrary to the principle of **anonymity** the founders and members have adopted.

AA began in a very quiet and personal way. One alcohol addict reached out to help another and help himself at the same time. It continues in this same **unobtrusive**, personal way even though the numbers have grown. In 1931, one of the founders sought help from the famous Swiss psychoanalyst, Carl Jung. He was told his only hope was in a vital spiritual experience. He went home and joined a religious group called the Oxford Movement. He shared with a friend the principles he was learning. They were: Admit you are beaten; Be honest with yourself; Talk your trouble out with someone; Make **restitution** to people you have harmed, and pray to God. Soon this friend was able to stop drinking, and so he, in turn, shared his experience with a fellow alcoholic.

This alcoholic could not accept the last point about praying because he did not believe in God. He tried. He prayed, "God, if there be a

God, let Him show Himself." Then he had a **psychic** experience. He tells it this way: "Suddenly the room lit up with a great white light. I was caught up in an ecstasy that no words can describe. It seemed to me in the mind's eye, that I was on a mountain, and that a wind not of air but of spirit was blowing. And then it burst upon me that I was a free man."

As a fellowship formed by alcoholics, Alcoholics Anonymous is an **autonomous** organization. It is run and supported by the members themselves. Its effectiveness in helping millions of alcohol addicts find a way to withdraw from the "spirited bottle" makes it a national, if not a world-wide model of alcoholic **rehabilitation.**

A. Each word or phrase below means the opposite of one of the new words in the lesson. On your paper, write the lesson word that is the antonym of the word listed. For help, reread the synonyms listed beside the lesson words on page 102 and notice how the words were used in the passage.

1. produced
2. popularity
3. non-payment
4. relapse
5. praise

6. dictatorial
7. noticeable
8. materialistic
9. destruction
10. quiet (celebration)

B. Look at each sentence below. Decide which answer is the opposite of the word in dark type in the sentence. Put your answers on your paper.

1. When you return stolen property, you make **restitution**.
   a. restoration
   b. no amends or payment
   c. a refund

2. The road signs were either **unobtrusive** or posted in places where nobody could easily see them.
   a. not noticeable
   b. noticeable
   c. missing

3. Few movie stars seek **anonymity**.
   a. recognition
   b. applause
   c. seclusion

4. Political candidates usually try to **debunk** their opponent's achievements.
   a. praise
   b. attack
   c. imitate

5. Graduation is usually celebrated with a great deal of **hoopla**.
   a. rehearsing
   b. stillness
   c. parties

6. Urban **renewal** has done much to improve people's lives
   a. rebuilding
   b. destruction
   c. reelection

C. Write a sentence to answer each question below. Use the lesson word in dark type in your answer.

1. What government effort, that you are aware of, shows its active support of non-profit groups aiding in the **rehabilitation** of former addicts?
2. Why do you, or don't you think an **autonomous** state is the ideal or perfect state?
3. Describe a **psychic** experience you have read or heard about.

Here are 10 facts you learned in Lessons 6–8. Ten lesson words are printed in dark type in the fact sentences. Match each lesson word with one synonym and one antonym from the lists below the sentences. Put your answers on your paper.

1. Each human being has a **unique** set of fingerprints.

2. Fingerprints fall in four general **configurations**.

3. Fingerprints give **incontestable** evidence of a person's identity.

4. The stories of the **ingenious** bride Sheherazade are called *The Arabian Nights*.

5. The caliph was **gullible** enough to believe that Sheherazade was too tired to finish her story.

6. All of the story plots in the collection are exciting and **intricate**.

7. Alcoholics Anonymous quietly passed on its message of spiritual **renewal** from one member to another.

8. To preserve its **autonomous** character, the organization has refused the financial aid of rich donors because they realize that "he who plays the piper calls the tune."

9. They avoid all the notoriety and **hoopla** that goes with many organizations.

10. **Anonymity** is the basic principle of Alcoholics Anonymous.

SYNONYMS		ANTONYMS	
believing	patterns	stupid	unproved
unquestionable	reform	ordinary	doubting
complicated	self-governing	simple	subordinate
clever	commotion	quiet	ruin
one of a kind	unknownness	fame	scatterings

For the items below, choose the word or phrase that means the same, or almost the same, as the word in dark type. Put your answers on your answer sheet. The test words come from Lessons 1–3.

Test Tips: Carefully read the phrase that contains the word in dark type. Decide if you have heard the phrase before. Then, read all four answers. Use your past knowledge to help you pick the best synonym.

1. **enhance** her appearance
   a. make
   b. improve
   c. ruin
   d. spoil

2. **attest** to his innocence
   a. object
   b. react
   c. witness
   d. challenge

3. **masticate** your food
   a. chew
   b. cook
   c. swallow
   d. eat

4. widely **acclaimed** comedian
   a. known
   b. criticized
   c. liked
   d. praised

5. a **destitute** person
   a. rich
   b. poor
   c. old
   d. radical

6. a strange **phenomenon**
   a. person
   b. noise
   c. happening
   d. place

7. a **celestial** being
   a. famous
   b. romantic
   c. real
   d. divine

8. brilliant **hues**
   a. lights
   b. people
   c. birds
   d. colors

9. **advantageous** situation
   a. lucky
   b. unfortunate
   c. lovely
   d. bad

10. **manifest** to everyone
    a. available
    b. evident
    c. nasty
    d. helpful

For items 11–20, choose the word or phrase that best completes the sentence. The key words in the sentences come from Lessons 4–5.

Test Tips: Reread the incomplete sentence carefully. Decide which word you are being asked to define in the sentence. This is the key word. Look for the answer choice that is a synonym of the key word.

11. If you surmise that what you hear is the truth, you __.
   a. do not know
   b. want to know
   c. guess
   d. doubt

12. When you domesticate an animal, you __ it.
   a. tame
   b. kill
   c. hit
   d. adopt

13. An unverified story is __.
   a. proven
   b. a lie
   c. amusing
   d. unproven

14. A legend about someone like Paul Bunyan is __.
   a. untrue
   b. partially true
   c. entirely true
   d. a fairy tale

15. A town devastated by floods has been __.
   a. surprised
   b. surrounded
   c. rebuilt
   d. destroyed

16. Dennis the Menace was a __ to his neighborhood.
   a. threat
   b. help
   c. joy
   d. asset

17. A deprecating remark is __.
   a. kind
   b. supportive
   c. critical
   d. funny

18. If a person reiterates a warning, he __.
   a. says it
   b. repeats it
   c. shouts it loudly
   d. whispers it

19. A competent worker knows his __.
   a. job
   b. friends
   c. income
   d. fellow workers

20. If you heed my advice, you __.
   a. ignore it
   b. hate it
   c. like it
   d. follow it

For items 21–30, choose the word that is most nearly the opposite of the word in dark type. Put your answers on your answer sheet. The test words come from Lessons 6–8.

Test Tips: Think of the meaning of the phrase. Then read all four answers carefully. Make sure you pick an antonym of the word in dark type.

21. **incontestable** fact
    a. simple
    b. known
    c. proven
    d. doubtful

22. **alleged** expert
    a. real
    b. so-called
    c. great
    d. questionable

23. **cognizant** of the subject
    a. ignorant
    b. knowledgeable
    c. aware
    d. afraid

24. **unique** house
    a. unusual
    b. different
    c. ordinary
    d. crazy

25. **intricate** pattern
    a. complex
    b. delicate
    c. simple
    d. pretty

26. **significant** moment
    a. important
    b. unimportant
    c. serious
    d. crucial

27. **enchanting** evening
    a. nice
    b. pleasant
    c. boring
    d. exciting

28. **psychic** phenomenon
    a. spiritual
    b. material
    c. strange
    d. sad

29. **restitution** for damages
    a. making payment
    b. making excuses
    c. making no payment
    d. making allowances

30. **autonomous** government
    a. self-ruling
    b. dependent
    c. dynamic
    d. democratic

For items 31–40, choose the answer that best completes each sentence. The test words come from Lessons 1–8.

Test Tips: Read all four answers carefully. Make sure you pick an antonym. Don't be tricked by a synonym or by a word that looks like the test word.

31. Hoopla is the opposite of __.
    a. silence
    b. funny
    c. noisy celebration
    d. quiet celebration

32. Prevalent is the opposite of __.
    a. unique
    b. common
    c. different
    d. ordinary

33. Loner is the opposite of __.
    a. lonely
    b. happy
    c. sociable
    d. unsociable

34. Bravado is the opposite of __.
    a. bravery
    b. cowardice
    c. brouhaha
    d. bravura

35. Obnoxious is the opposite of __.
    a. horrid
    b. hateful
    c. lonely
    d. pleasant

36. Dissembling is the opposite of __.
    a. not knowing
    b. pretending
    c. not concealing
    d. concealing

37. Cultivate is the opposite of __.
    a. grow
    b. lose
    c. destroy
    d. make

38. Viscous is the opposite of __.
    a. free flowing
    b. sticky
    c. non-flowing
    d. molasses

39. Pragmatic is the opposite of __.
    a. practical
    b. useful
    c. realistic
    d. idealistic

40. Unassuming is the opposite of __.
    a. boastful
    b. shy
    c. smart
    d. modest

PART 2

Context Clues

In Part 2, you will learn a way to make a logical guess about the meaning of a new word you meet in your reading. You will learn to look for meaning clues within the sentences and paragraphs that you read. You will learn to notice how a new word is used and to relate the new word to other words or ideas in the reading. This technique will help you figure out the meaning of the new word.

Look at the picture below. The picture illustrates the meaning of the word **crimp**. Look for clues in the picture to help you figure out the meaning of the word **crimp**. Write your guess on your paper.

Suppose you come across an unfamiliar word in your reading. You can make a good guess about the word's meaning, even without looking in a dictionary. You can look for meaning clues in the words and sentences that come before and after the new word. The meaning clues you can locate near a new word are called *context clues*.

Practice using context clues to help you figure out the meaning of **requisite** in the following paragraph about food. The ideas mentioned before and after **requisite** will help you define it. Write your guess on your paper.

Certain foods are necessary to the growth and good health of human beings all over the world. Nature seems to have a way of supplying these foods wherever humans live. Grains are probably the first food **requisite**. Next on the list would be proteins, fruits, vegetables, and dairy products. In America, we are fortunate to have adequate samples of these basic foods from every part of the world.

Check your answer. Think about what you read. You know that certain foods are needed. The word *necessary* is used in the first sentence. These clues help you know **requisite** means "necessary."

You should look for different kinds of context clues when you read to help you define unfamiliar words.

CLUE 1: DEFINITION CLUE

Sometimes you will find the meaning of a new word given right before or after a word. The definition will be in the same sentence. Find a definition clue below to help you know what **indigenous** means.

We think of wheat as being the staple in our diet. From wheat comes the bread, pasta, and cereal that we eat every day. The basic raw ingredient for America's favorite pizza is wheat. But in countries where wheat is not **indigenous** or native to the soil and climate, people have learned to prefer rice. This is the food staple of the countries of Southeast Asia.

Check your answer. The words *or native* come right after **indigenous**. They tell you **indigenous** means "native."

CLUE 2: SERIES CLUE

Sometimes a new word will be part of a group of words that go together. You can figure out the meaning of the new word by studying the other words in the series. Use a series clue to help you know what **legumes** means in the paragraph below.

Vegetables are a necesary source of vitamins. A favorite vegetable in Europe and America, is the potato. If you disagree, think of the popularity of *French Fries,* or *Pomme Frites,* as called in Europe. Peas, beans, peanuts, and other **legumes** follow as international favorites.

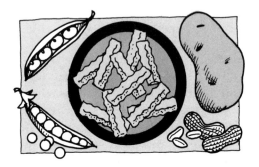

Check your answer. Legumes is in a series of names for plants producing edible seeds. You can guess that **legumes** are such plants.

CLUE 3: SYNONYM CLUE

Sometimes you can spot a synonym of an unfamiliar word in a sentence near the one in which the new word appears. Look for a synonym in the paragraph below to help you define the word **nomenclature**.

Our favorite fruit is the apple. Actually, apples belong to the rose family. The sweet smell of apple blossoms in the spring might suggest that to us. The family name is *Rosacea.* There are wild varieties of Rosacea, but those we are familiar with are the cultivated ones. The **nomenclature** for the domestic species of apple is *Malus Domestica.* Apple is an Old English word for this ancient fruit.

Check your answer. In the paragraph, the word *name* is used two sentences before the sentence with the new word **nomenclature**. You can tell **nomenclature** means "name."

CLUE 4: ANTONYM CLUE

Sometimes you can spot an antonym of a new word in a sentence near the sentence in which the new word appears. The antonym can help you define the unfamiliar word. Look for an antonym below to help you guess what **frugality** means.

Meat dishes, especially beefsteaks and hamburgers, are the Americans' favorite sources of protein. Many other countries consider Americans extravagant in their choice of protein-rich food. The Swiss, known for their **frugality**, get more protein from cheese than from beefsteak.

Check your answer. You can tell from the passage that *extravagant* is the opposite of **frugality**. So **frugality** must mean "thrifty."

CLUE 5: EXPERIENCE CLUE

Sometimes you can guess the meaning of an unfamiliar word because the meaning makes sense to you. The meaning fits with things you know to be true about a subject. Use your experience to guess the meaning of **quintessential** in the following paragraph.

Another food category is dairy products. We all need milk. Most people like eggs, butter, and cheese. But it is ice cream that is the **quintessential** American favorite dairy product. Some like the simple chocolate or vanilla varieties. Others crave for the chocolate truffle and Dom Perignon gourmet flavors sold in San Francisco for $50 a pint. Ice cream is the dessert for the rich and poor, for the old and young.

Check your answer. You know ice cream is the tops in our choice of desserts. Therefore, you can guess that **quintessential** means the "most typical" or the "most essential."

LESSON 1

Here are the eight new words in this lesson. Their meanings are not listed. Look for the new words in the passage below. Try to find context clues to help you define the new words. You will find some hints to help you in the questions on the next page.

prone   **aerated**   **vitalized**   **pensive**
alienate   **alleviate**   **reflect**   **harried**

The Perfect Pet

The turtle is the perfect pet for the nervous, Type A personality (as certain excitable, heart-attack-**prone** individuals are called today). Turtles do not bark or screech and otherwise **alienate** the neighbors. They do not get fleas on their body, that fall in the carpet. They do not scratch up the upholstery. They do not smell. They do not have to have their water changed or **aerated**, and they do not eat up expensive and colorful smaller fish. They do not scatter birdseed all over the living room.

If members of a family tend to argue over who is to pet the pet, a turtle can **alleviate** that problem. Nobody wants to pet a turtle! Even when you feel exhausted, just watching a turtle lying in a box can make you feel more **vitalized** than he looks.

But if you **reflect** on it, the real advantage of the turtle as a pet comes when you are not in a pet-caring mood because there are too many other things that must get done. Then you will notice that the turtle's principal occupation is sleeping in the sun. It just lies there and lets the world race by. It never frets. And when it does rouse itself to taste a bit of pumpkin or sip some water, the turtle proceeds very, very slowly. Just watching it will put you in a calm, **pensive** mood. You find yourself thinking, "Ah, that's why turtles live to be over 100."

So, when you are very busy and feeling particularly **harried**, you might say like the Mock Turtle in *Alice in Wonderland*, "We call him tortoise because he taught us."

114

A. Each question below asks you to use a context clue to help you determine the meaning of one of the new words in the passage on page 114. Write your answers on your paper.

1. The word **prone** is used with "heart attack" as part of an adjective. It helps you guess that **prone** means ___.
   a. inclined
   b. disposed
   c. both a and b

2. Find **alienate** in the passage. Words in the same sentence help you guess **alienate** means ___.
   a. to please people
   b. to get people interested
   c. to make people unfriendly

3. You can tell from the passage that **aerated** has something to do with water. It means ___.
   a. to put air into water
   b. to color water
   c. to wash something

4. Find **alleviate** in the passage. It is used with the word *problem* You can guess **alleviate** means ___.
   a. help solve a problem
   b. be responsible for a problem
   c. cause a problem

5. Find **vitalized** in the story. What antonym for **vitalized** is found in the same sentence?
   a. exhausted
   b. lying
   c. watching

6. The words before and after **reflect** help you know that **reflect** means ___.
   a. think
   b. ignore
   c. crawl

7. The word that comes first in the series with **pensive** helps you guess that **pensive** means ___.
   a. thoughtful
   b. excited
   c. worried

8. **Harried** is also in a series. This series suggests that **harried** means ___.
   a. slow and easy
   b. gentle and kind
   c. hurried and anxious

B. Look back over your answers in Activity A to find synonyms for the new words. On your paper, list the lesson words and your synonyms.

C. Write a sentence to answer each question below. Use the lesson word in dark type in your answer.

1. What can we do to **alleviate** the sufferings of children in the world?
2. What surroundings are most likely to put you in a **pensive** mood?
3. At what time of the day do you feel most **vitalized** and lively?

LESSON 2

Here are the eight new words in this lesson. Their meanings are not listed. Look for these new words in the story below. Try to find context clues to help you define the lesson words. You will find some hints to help you in the questions on the next page.

| unpretentious | perplexities | therapy | debilitating |
| superseded | subjected (to) | incomprehensible | visualize |

Olympic Champion

Handsome Greg Louganis is probably the most outstanding diver in the entire world. At the 1984 Los Angeles Olympics, his perfect, graceful dives filled the watching world with wonder. He was the first American in 56 years to win both the 3-meter and the 10-meter diving competitions. This quiet, modest, and **unpretentious** young man first achieved the highest point count in the history of diving—688.5. Then he **superseded** that with an incredible 710.9 points.

The trials and **perplexities** of his childhood probably served to build his determination. First of all, as the adopted son of a Samoan father, he attended an all-white school where he was **subjected** to name-calling and prejudice. He also stuttered and had to take speech **therapy** classes to overcome this problem. In addition, unknown to him and to his teachers, he had *dyslexia*. Dyslexia is a reading disability that, among other things, makes words like "but" look like "tub" and "star" look like "rats." What he read became **incomprehensible**. His teachers, not realizing the problem, called him lazy. All this was embarrassing to Greg and could have been **debilitating**, but instead, it gave him a great drive to force himself to be strong, and to overcome these handicaps.

By the time he was 16 years old and in high school, he brought home the silver medal from the Montreal Olympics. This was a surprise to his fellow students. In addition to three Olympic medals, he has also won 35 National Championships.

Today, after years of reaching for the goals he had set for himself, Greg Louganis has all the self-confidence he needs. He can truly **visualize** himself in his own mind as the public sees him: a champion!

A. Each question below asks you to use a context clue to help you determine the meaning of one of the new words used in the story on page 116. Write your answers on your paper.

1. Find the word **unpretentious**. The preceding words in the series help you guess that **unpretentious** means not __.
   a. proud
   b. humble
   c. wise

2. The fact that 710.9 is more than 688.5 helps you guess that **superseded** means __.
   a. went beyond
   b. undercut
   c. equaled

3. The grouping of **perplexities** with *trials* helps you know **perplexities** also means __.
   a. games
   b. confusions
   c. ideas

4. The words right after **subjected (to)** — help you guess **subjected (to)** means __.
   a. caused to undergo
   b. frightened by
   c. pleased by

5. Since *dyslexia* is a reading problem, you can guess that **incomprehensible** means __.
   a. very easy
   b. not understandable
   c. too difficult

6. Find **debilitating** in the story. A synonym in the same sentence helps you guess that **debilitating** means __.
   a. strengthening
   b. encouraging
   c. weakening

7. The words *in his own mind* should help you to guess that **visualize** means to __.
   a. know
   b. imagine
   c. hear

8. The words in the same sentence with **therapy** help you guess that **therapy** is a form of __.
   a. treatment
   b. talent
   c. medicine

B. Look back over your answers in Activity A to find synonyms for the new words. On your paper, list the lesson words and their synonyms.

C. Write a sentence to answer each question below. Use the lesson word in dark type in your sentence.

1. How do you **visualize** yourself ten years from now?
2. What are some **perplexities** young people face today?
3. What kind of reading do you find **incomprehensible**?

LESSON 3

Here are the eight new words in this lesson. Their meanings are not listed. Look for the new words in the passage below. Try to find context clues to help you define the lesson words. You will find some hints to help you in the questions on the next page.

| harmony | ethereal | melancholy | inscrutable |
| novel | predilection | vibrate | disparate |

The Oldest Musical Instrument

Like a lovely fragrance floating in and out of memory, comes the song of the wind harp. It is a haunting **harmony** of sounds, played by the mysterious hand of the wind moving across guitar-like strings or wires. Creating these new harps has become a **novel** art form.

The harp is the oldest of all musical instruments. A Sumerian harp found by archeologists, is thought to be over 4,500 years old. According to the Bible, Jubal invented the harp. King David played the harp and used it as he composed psalms.

The Aeolian harp, as the wind harp is called, was apparently inspired by other hanging harps. It takes its name from the Greek god of the wind, Aeolus, probably because it seems as if some mysterious, **ethereal** hand is moving the strings. The people of the 1800's who had a **predilection** or taste for romance and **melancholy**, used to hang a box-like harp in a window or some place where it would catch the breeze. It was usually a long, thin wooden box to which 8 to 15 fine strings or wires were attached at each end. The strings stretched tightly over low bridges (much like guitar or violin bridges). The wind caused the strings to **vibrate**, and their quivering produced a natural, yet **inscrutable** melody which was as beautiful as it was mysterious.

Today, wind harps come in all shapes and sizes. Ross Barable has a shop in North Carolina where he has a 10½-foot wind harp and a "soundiferous" garden in the mountains where people can go to hear the beautiful sounds. The Buchens together with other artists in Lake Placid, New York, have made a harp which covers four acres. Another harp, which sits on top of California's Candlestick Point State Park, looks like a giant 20-foot toadstool or umbrella. These incredible harps are as **disparate** from the folk harps and concert harps we know, as from the 19th-century Aeolian harp.

118

A. Each question below asks you to use a context clue to help you determine the meaning of one of the new words used in the passage on page 118. Write your answers on your paper.

1. Find **harmony** in the passage. The word *lovely* in the same paragraph helps you guess that **harmony** means __.
   a. loud sounds
   b. pleasing sounds
   c. clashing sounds

2. Find the word **novel** in the first paragraph. What synonym for **novel** is used to describe harps?
   a. creating
   b. new
   c. thrilling

3. The word *mysterious* right before **ethereal** helps you know **ethereal** means __.
   a. ordinary and common
   b. strange and otherworldly
   c. loud and angry

4. The phrase right after **predilection** shows you that **predilection** means __.
   a. a taste or liking
   b. a dislike or hatred
   c. an acknowledgement

5. *Romance* and **melancholy** are in the same sentence. You can guess that **melancholy** is __.
   a. a lively song
   b. an imaginative person
   c. a tender feeling

6. You know that strings must move to make sounds. You can guess **vibrate** means __.
   a. to quiver
   b. to break
   c. to stop

7. In the passage, *natural* is contrasted with **inscrutable**. Therefore, **inscrutable** means __.
   a. common
   b. beautiful
   c. mysterious

8. Since the modern wind harps do not look anything like the old harps, you can guess that **disparate** means __.
   a. similar
   b. new
   c. different

B. Look back over your answers in Activity A to find synonyms for the new words. On your paper, list the new words and their synonyms.

C. Write a sentence to answer each question below. Use the lesson word in dark type in your sentence.

1. On a guitar, how are **vibrations** of the strings made louder?
2. How many people in this class have a **predilection** for rock music?
3. How many **disparate** types of music can you name?

LESSON 4

Here are the eight new words in this lesson. Their meanings are not given. Look for the new words in the passage below. Try to find context clues to help you define the new words. You will find some hints to help you in the questions on the next page.

tentatively	**endeavor**	**inhibited**	**apartheid**
interfaith	**stereotype**	**diversity**	**tolerance**

A School for Feelings

On an ordinary day in a small village in Israel, a group of high school students **tentatively** or hesitantly enter a school called *Neve Shalom* to begin the day's classes. What makes this school very different from others, is that its students are Arabs and Jews. They comprise an **interfaith** community of Christian Arabs, Moslem Arabs, and Jews struggling to coexist peacefully in the heart of war-torn Middle East.

The main work of the school is to conduct classes and workshops for students from Arab and Jewish high schools. When they arrive, the teenagers are divided into discussion groups—one led by a Jew, another by an Arab. The Jew speaks in Hebrew while the Arab translates into Arabic. The students begin by naming things they like. Then they **endeavor** to repeat each other's name and recall each other's favorite objects. They try to break through the **stereotype** they have of each other, by shedding fixed ideas of each other, and by realizing that each of them is a different and special person.

When the groups break up, the leaders ask for reports on the discussions. The students are **inhibited** at first, but then they courageously begin to reveal what they have remembered about one another. Who is not allowed to have girlfriends until he is 21; which one likes Arabic poetry; who prefers to listen to popular music? Through this dialogue, the students gradually put prejudices aside.

Unlike the United States where a **diversity** of people of different races, religions, and political beliefs live and work together, Israel and the Arab countries have tried to prevent their respective societies from being influenced by the other. Neither culture supports integrated schools, or approves of intermarriage. At best, each culture tries to achieve a middle ground between integration and **apartheid**. Someday maybe, students of schools like Neve Shalom may enjoin their people to face differences with **tolerance** and move toward peaceful coexistence.

A. Each question below asks you to use a context clue to help you determine the meaning of one of the new words used in the passage on page 120. Write your answers on your paper.

1. Find **tentatively** in the story. What synonym for **tentatively** is used in the same paragraph?
   a. ordinary
   b. hesitantly
   c. struggling

2. The words in the series with **interfaith** help you guess an **interfaith** community is made up of people of __.
   a. the same religions
   b. different religions
   c. different nationalities

3. Find **endeavor** in the story. What synonym for **endeavor** is used in the next sentence?
   a. try
   b. break
   c. recall

4. Words after **stereotype** help you guess **stereotype** means a __.
   a. bad impression
   b. good impression
   c. fixed impression

5. An antonym used in the same sentence with **inhibited** helps you know **inhibited** means __.
   a. fearful
   b. courageous
   c. remembered

6. The words with **diversity** help you guess **diversity** means __.
   a. similarity
   b. division
   c. variety

7. An antonym used in the sentence with **apartheid** hints that **apartheid** means living __.
   a. with others
   b. without a home
   c. apart from others

8. The purpose of Neve Shalom is to help students understand each other's backgrounds. You guess **tolerance** means __.
   a. putting up with something
   b. fighting something
   c. studying something

B. Look back over your answers in Activity A to find synonyms for the new words. On your paper, list the lesson words and their synonyms.

C. Write a sentence to answer each question below. Use the lesson word in dark type in your sentence.

1. What **stereotype** do many people have of teenagers?
2. What might **inhibit** others from tolerating people of different cultures?
3. What can you **endeavor** to do to help prevent racial prejudice?

Here are 10 facts you have learned in the four lessons in Part 2. One word has been omitted from each fact sentence. Decide which choice below the sentence best fills the blank. Then write the completed sentence on your paper.

1. Pet animals that make loud noises tend to ___ the neighbors.

aerate   visualize   alienate

2. Watching how animals behave can put you in a ___ mood.

prone   pensive   debilitating

3. A good time to stop and reflect on things is when you are rushed and ___.

inhibited   alleviated   harried

4. Greg Louganis is a champion who ___ his own diving record.

superseded   alienated   visualized

5. He is a modest and ___ champion.

harried   pensive   unpretentious

6. He did not let the ___ of his youth prevent him from achieving his goals.

endeavor   predilection   perplexities

7. The strings of wind harps ___ in the wind.

aerate   reflect   vibrate

8. Wind harps create a mysterious and ___ sound.

diverse   inscrutable   unpretentious

9. Neve Shalom in Israel is an ___ community.

interfaith   apartheid   inhibited

10. The students of Neve Shalom ___ to overcome their stereotype images of one another.

supersede   reflect   endeavor

TAKING TESTS

Choose the word or phrase that means the same, or almost the same, as the word in dark type in each item below. Put your answers on your answer sheet. The test words come from Lessons 1–2.

Test Tips: Some answer choices are put in a test to trick you. Make sure you pick a synonym for the word in dark type. Don't pick an answer that fits in the phrase but is not a synonym of the test word.

1. **alleviate** the suffering
   a. increase
   b. lessen
   c. stop
   d. create

2. a **harried** student
   a. happy
   b. rushed
   c. silly
   d. brilliant

3. **alienate** his affections
   a. break off
   b. increase
   c. pursue
   d. desire

4. **prone** to evil
   a. resigned
   b. used
   c. inclined
   d. opposed

5. a **pensive** look
   a. thoughtful
   b. foolish
   c. good
   d. deceitful

6. prescribed **therapy**
   a. remedy
   b. diet
   c. penalty
   d. reward

7. the **perplexities** of life
   a. joys
   b. confusions
   c. sorrows
   d. solutions

8. a **debilitating** disease
   a. slight
   b. weakening
   c. curable
   d. common

9. **reflect** on the problem
   a. meditate
   b. lecture
   c. debate
   d. decide

10. **subject** to criticism
    a. respond
    b. blind
    c. objecting
    d. open

Choose the word or phrase that means the same, or almost the same, as the word in dark type in each sentence below. Put your answers on your answer sheet. The test words come from Lessons 3–4.

Test Tips: Use the sentence context to help you. Try to put the answer choice in the place of the word in dark type. Decide if the sentence still has the same meaning.

11. Tom and his sister have very **disparate** life-styles.
    a. similar
    b. different
    c. unusual
    d. strange

12. Many young people have a **predilection** for rock music.
    a. distaste
    b. talent
    c. liking
    d. concern

13. Guitar strings **vibrate** to make musical sounds.
    a. stretch
    b. swing
    c. move
    d. break

14. An **ethereal** music came from the harp on the mountain.
    a. loud
    b. soft
    c. unearthly
    d. ugly

15. Intelligent persons **endeavor** to understand other people's points of view.
    a. try
    b. pretend
    c. like
    d. hate

16. Ignorance can **inhibit** one from reaching out to people of different cultures.
    a. encourage
    b. prevent
    c. discourage
    d. distract

17. **Diversity** is a characteristic of American society.
    a. materialism
    b. intolerance
    c. tolerance
    d. variety

18. A **tentative** attempt is better than no attempt.
    a. faltering
    b. hostile
    c. willing
    d. foolish

Read the selection below. Notice the words in dark type. Choose the word that best answers each question below the selection.

Test Tips: Read the sentence that contains each test word carefully. Look for a context clue in the sentence or the sentences near it. Make a logical guess about the meaning of the test word. Then see if your guess is similar to one of the answers.

In 1976, when most Swiss watch makers were struggling to survive in a threatened industry, Raymond Weil, a Swiss, started a new watch company. His idea seemed quite sensible and admirable to the American mind. To the Swiss, on the other hand, his idea seemed **reprehensible**.

First, instead of creating an expensive, once-in-a-lifetime timepiece, Weil designed an inexpensive fashion accessory to be worn as part of a wardrobe. His watches were made of inexpensive metal, leather or vinyl and came in **diverse** styles and colors—pink, blue, black, etc. That way, people would want to own several watches to match a variety of outfits.

His next **innovation** was to avoid showing his watches in the **prestigious** or snobbish catalogs. Instead, he advertised all over the world in such **unpretentious** places as posters on buses, TV commercials, and popular magazines. His business **acumen** paid off. His company was so successful that other companies are now following his example.

---

19. What does **reprehensible** mean in the selection?
a. admirable   c. new
b. worthless   d. old

20. What does **diverse** mean in the selection?
a. common   c. varied
b. bright   d. dull

21. What is an **innovation**?
a. trip   c. new idea
b. thought   d. expense

22. What does **prestigious** mean in the selection?
a. powerful   c. poor
b. impressive   d. local

23. What does **unpretentious** mean in the selection?
a. simple   c. rare
b. snobbish   d. unreal

24. What does **acumen** mean in the selection?
a. skill   c. shrewdness
b. sharpness   d. a, b, and c

PART 3 *Words with Several Meanings*

The new words you are going to learn in Part 3 each have several different meanings. However, only one of the meanings will fit the way the word is used in the reading selection. You will be able to determine which meaning fits by using context clues to define the new words.

Look at the three pictures below. Each picture illustrates a different meaning of the same word. Can you guess what the secret word is? Do you know all three meanings of the word?

A single word can have several different meanings. You can find all of the meanings listed in a dictionary entry for the word. You need to look carefully at how the word is used in a sentence or paragraph to determine which meaning fits in the reading.

Look at the four sentences below. The word *look* appears in each one. In each sentence, *look* has a different meaning.

1. At a railroad crossing, stop, look, and listen.
2. It feels good to be a strong youth who can look after the weak and aging.
3. You can look forward to being somebody, someday—after years of hard work.
4. Look into the problem carefully, before you decide on a solution.

Here are four different definitions of the word *look*. Each meaning fits the way the word was used in one of the sentences you just read. On your paper, indicate which meaning fits in each sentence.

a. investigate or probe
b. care for or attend to the needs of someone
c. to expect or hope for something
d. see with your eyes

Check your answers. Note how *look* was used in each sentence. The correct matches are 1. **d**, 2. **b**, 3. **c**, 4. **a**.

Think about other words that have several meanings. How many different meanings can you think of for each of the following words? Write down your meanings. Then look up each word in a dictionary to find additional meanings.

trade	rank
fine	rose
serve	raise
right	range
play	canon

Do the activities on the next two pages. You will learn more about choosing the meaning of a word that fits in the reading.

A. Read the following paragraph about a famous novel and movie written by E.M. Forster.

Passage to India is an 18th-century novel that was made into an award-winning movie. It is about two English women who travel to India. They face difficulties when they become involved with an Indian man who tries to be helpful to them.

Here are three meanings of **passage**. Which meaning do you think would apply to E.M. Forster's story?

1. a short part of a speech or reading
2. a narrow hallway or pathway
3. a journey

Check your answer. You should have picked the meaning in **3**.

B. One word is printed in dark type in each selection below about a well-known story. Decide which meaning below the selection fits the way the key word is used. Put your answers on your paper.

1. *Huckleberry Finn* is a story about a boy who sailed down the Mississippi River on a **raft**. He and his friend Jim had many adventures.
   a. a small craft made of wooden logs or boards which rides on the water
   b. a large collection of things or people

2. One of the best novels (and movies) about the **Depression** Era was *The Grapes of Wrath* by John Steinbeck. It is about the Joad family who migrated to the west when they lost their farm.
   a. a tropical storm that does not move toward land
   b. a period of economic trouble when business is terrible

3. The novel, *The Great Gatsby,* was first written as a short story for a **magazine**.
   a. a storage place for ammunition
   b. a periodical

4. Shakespeare's play, *Othello,* is about a **Moor** named Othello, who murders his beautiful wife, Desdemona.
   a. boggy area of wasteland
   b. an inhabitant of what is now Morocco in North Africa

Check your answers. You should have picked **a** for 1, **b** for 2, **b** for 3, and **b** for 4.

C. Here are the kinds of questions that you sometimes see on a reading test. Read the meaning printed at the top of each item. Then find the sentence in which the word in dark type has the same meaning. Put your answers on your paper.

1. the floors in a building
   a. She told ghost **stories** to the children on Halloween.
   b. The top **stories** are all expensive penthouses.

2. the beach of a sea
   a. The lovers walked along the **strand** in the twilight.
   b. She wove a **strand** of gold thread into the embroidery.

3. a group of living cells
   a. I have such a cold, that I used a whole box of **tissues**.
   b. After the accident, the torn **tissues** of her ankle healed slowly.

4. legal proof of ownership of property
   a. I received the **title** to my car after I paid off the loan.
   b. What is the **title** of the book we have to read for our English class?

5. the sound of a bell
   a. We had to pay a **toll** of $5 to cross that bridge.
   b. As the bell began to **toll**, the people gathered in the town square.

6. small gift
   a. Dan **favors** his grandfather. He, too, has an easygoing disposition.
   b. Each child received a balloon as a party **favor**.

Check your answers. You should have picked **b** for 1, **a** for 2, **b** for 3, **a** for 4, **b** for 5, and **b** for 6.

Here are the eight new words in this lesson. Each lesson word has several different meanings. You will need to use context clues from the passage to help you determine the meaning that fits in the passage.

plague   paraphernalia
launch   canteen
raging   stalwart
inaccessible   dispatch

Smoke Jumpers

Between May and October when forest fires **plague** many parts of the country, a courageous band of men and women called smoke jumpers are called upon to rescue the wilderness. They are based at five main forestry stations in Alaska, Oregon, California, Montana, and Idaho where they **launch** their operations aboard rescue planes.

The smoke jumpers drop down into **raging** fires that are miles from civilization. There they dig trenches, cut down trees, and pinch off sections of the fire until they get it under control and stop it from further spreading. Most of these fires have been sparked by lightning striking the tall timbers in rugged country that is **inaccessible** except by air.

The **paraphernalia** the smoke jumpers must jump with include about 125 pounds of tools (shovels, forest axes, chain saws, cross-cut saws, climbing spurs), a gallon of water, two days' supply of freeze-dried food, a radio, and a sleeping bag. In addition, they have a parachute canopy which is a padded white suit with a reserve canopy attached, and a rope to be used in case they get caught in the trees and have to swing down to the ground. They also carry a hard hat, a coat, and a **canteen**. All of this equipment must be retrieved when the fire has been put out.

These **stalwart** men and women come from all walks of life, and most have other careers. The basic requirements are physical fitness and at least two and a half years of fire-fighting experience. The physical fitness admittance test includes 45 sit-ups, 25 push-ups, 7 pull-ups, and one mile and a half run in less than 11 minutes. Then their training begins. This includes trampoline work, rope- and pole-climbing, practice parachute-jumping, and first aid. Several have an Emergency Medical Technician license. Also, many are trained in computer work so that they can get instant information on fire locations, weather, and where to **dispatch** the jumpers.

The job of a smoke jumper is dangerous, demanding, exhausting, and low-paying. Still, it creates a special kind of hero, someone who combines a love of the outdoors with both daring and dedication.

A. The new words in Lesson 1 are listed below. After each lesson word are two of its meanings. Decide which meaning fits the way the word is used in the passage. Put your answers on your paper.

1. plague
   a. cause trouble
   b. deadly disease

2. launch
   a. set off
   b. small motorboat

3. raging
   a. angry
   b. spreading

4. inaccessible
   a. impossible to obtain
   b. impossible to reach

5. paraphernalia
   a. personal belongings
   b. equipment

6. canteen
   a. covered water bottle
   b. a refreshment bar

7. stalwart
   a. fearless
   b. faithful

8. dispatch
   a. kill
   b. send off

B. The words below are synonyms of four of the new words in this lesson. Write down the new lesson word that matches the synonym.

1. brave
2. supplies

3. start
4. annoy

C. Write a sentence to answer each question below. Use the lesson word in dark type in your sentence.

1. What **paraphernalia** do you need for the beach?
2. Name one entertainer who plays the role of a **stalwart** character.
3. Which local official do you find to be the most **inaccessible**?

Here are the eight new words in this lesson. Each lesson word has several different meanings. You will need to use context clues from the passage to help you determine the meaning that fits in the passage.

favored	curiosity
lumbering	rare
innocence	amber
present	appreciation

Zoo Favorites

Anyone might guess the most **favored** animals in the zoo are the graceful lions and tigers. But if you ask zoo keepers, that is not the case. It is the frolicsome monkey, the **lumbering** bear and friendly marine mammals that people love most. The reason, according to Erica Beck, an animal trainer, is that these animals remind us of the **innocence** which we leave behind in childhood. Most animals are simple. They do what they were created to do—eat, sleep, and reproduce. They don't steal unless they need food. They don't kill what they can't eat, or what they don't suspect is about to kill them. So most people are at least fond of one kind of animal or another.

In the Denver Zoo is Rok, an orangutan (monkey), who looks a little like "Curious George," a favorite storybook character known to many children.

Two of the most famous animals in the country are Ling Ling and her mate, Hsing Hsing. They are the Giant Panda bears in the National Zoo in Washington, D.C. They were a **present** from the People's Republic of China in honor of President Nixon's visit there in 1972. They are a **curiosity**, not only because they are **rare**, but also because they are also the objects of great sympathy and affection. People waited many years for the cuddly-looking, black-eyed couple to have babies. They had one born dead and one that died shortly after

birth. Pandas do not seem able to have offspring easily, and the American public reacted with sympathy for the cub-wanting Ling Ling and Hsing Hsing.

Then there is an old walrus at the Brooklyn Zoo. Her name is Olga. Born in 1961, she has big **amber** eyes and a pale amber mustache. She is too leathery and wet to be cuddly, but she loves people and shows it. They wave and yell, and she waves back, spouts water, and blows kisses in **appreciation** for their affection. Apparently, even animals have their fans!

A. The new words in Lesson 2 are listed below. After each lesson word are two of its meanings. Decide which meaning fits the way the word was used in the passage. Put your answers on your paper.

1. **favored**
   a. preferred
   b. gifted

2. **lumbering**
   a. involved in cutting trees
   b. walking clumsily

3. **innocence**
   a. simple nature
   b. ignorance

4. **present**
   a. gift
   b. in attendance

5. **curiosity**
   a. desire to know
   b. something odd

6. **rare**
   a. half-cooked
   b. unusual

7. **amber**
   a. a jewel made from resin
   b. deep yellow

8. **appreciation**
   a. increase in value
   b. gratitude

B. The words below are synonyms of the new words in this lesson. Write down the lesson word that matches each synonym.

1. uncommon
2. moving awkwardly
3. simplicity
4. gratitude

C. Write a sentence to answer each question below. Use the lesson word in dark type in your sentence.

1. What occasion do you feel calls for a letter of **appreciation**?
2. What animals generally have **amber** eyes?
3. Which film or story of a recording star's private life has excited the public's **curiosity**?

Here are the ten new words in this lesson. Each word has several meanings. You will need to use context clues from the passage to help you determine the meaning that fits in the passage.

auspices	grip
sage	gull
race	rigid
seal	blanket
unctuous	skinning

Arctic Olympics

Every July, the natives of our 49th state gather in Fairbanks, under the **auspices** of the Fairbanks Chamber of Commerce, to compete in their own version of the Olympic games. The games were originally started by the elderly **sage** of the community. They thought of competitions that will help prepare their youth for the harsh life of the Arctic. The competitors were at first all Eskimos, but later, the games were expanded to include the native American Indian tribes.

The Olympics open with a torch **race**. The runners cover a five-kilometer (three-mile) course, and the winner carries the torch in a ceremonial race. After this run, the torch is used to light two lamps. One lamp has **seal** oil to represent the Eskimos. The other lamp has an **unctuous** liquid of moose tallow or fat to represent the Indians.

One of the first events is a man versus woman tug-of-war. Eskimo and Indian women are generally tiny, but they can **grip** with great strength and endurance. The men of the audience are invited to join, and though they may outnumber and outweigh the 50 or so women, the women always win.

The "Arm Pull" is something like what we call Indian wrestling or arm wrestling. The athletes lock arms at the elbows and each tries to pull the other toward him. Sometimes one tries to **gull** the other by pretending to weaken.

The most difficult event, perhaps, is the "Drop the Bomb" competition. The athlete lies on the floor, arms and legs stiff, spread-eagle fashion. Three men carry him in this position while he maintains his **rigid** pose as long as he can. When he sags and his body touches the ground, the distance is measured. The record is 263 feet.

For fun, there is the "**Blanket** Toss." Once it was used to throw a hunter as high as possible so that he could try to spot whales on the horizon. They toss a man as high as 40 feet. Today, the blanket is made of walrus skins and is pulled by many men in a wavy motion. The athlete tries to land on his feet on the blanket each time and go higher and higher while he does tricks.

Other events include **skinning** seal, folk dancing, and a beauty contest.

A. The new words in Lesson 3 are listed below. After each lesson word are two of its meanings. Decide which meaning fits the way the word was used in the passage. Put your answers on your paper.

1. **auspices**
   a. prophetic signs
   b. sponsorship

2. **sage**
   a. wise person
   b. a plant of the mint family

3. **race**
   a. a competition
   b. a tribe or nation

4. **seal**
   a. an animal
   b. to close up

5. **unctuous**
   a. rich in fat and oil
   b. insincere

6. **grip**
   a. handle
   b. hold firmly

7. **gull**
   a. a sea bird
   b. to take advantage of

8. **rigid**
   a. precise or accurate
   b. stiff or inflexible

9. **blanket**
   a. a material covering a bed
   b. covering a whole area

10. **skinning**
    a. taking the skin from
    b. cheating

B. The words below are synonyms of four of the new words in the lesson. Write down the lesson word that matches each synonym.

1. trick
2. tournament
3. learned person
4. stiff

C. Write a sentence to answer each question below. Use the lesson word in dark type in your answer.

1. What would a **blanket** insurance policy cover?
2. Under whose **auspices** is the Summer Olympics?
3. What is one scheme that is used to **gull** consumers?

Here are 10 facts you have learned in Lessons 1–3 of Part 3. The words written in italics in the fact sentences are synonyms of the 10 lesson words listed at the bottom of this page. Rewrite the sentences, using the lesson words to replace the synonyms.

1. In fighting forest fires, some personnel are trained in computer work that helps determine where to *send* smoke jumpers.

2. Smoke jumpers carry over 100 pounds of *equipment* on their jumps.

3. Fires are a *calamity* in any forest.

4. Walruses have bright *yellow* eyes.

5. They spout watery kisses in *gratitude* for the public's affection.

6. Most people love animals because animals remind them of the *simplicity* of childhood.

7. Pandas are an exotic and *unusual* animal.

8. The *wise elder* among the Eskimos devised games to train the young for a hard life.

9. The lamp representing the Indians is fueled by a *fatty* substance that is basically moose tallow.

10. The hardest Arctic Olympic game is the one which requires a player to remain *stiff* while being carried.

LESSON WORDS

amber   plague
paraphernalia   rare
sage   rigid
innocence   dispatch
appreciation   unctuous

Choose the sentence in which the word in dark type means the same as the definition given. Put your answers on your answer sheet.

Test Tips: Try to substitute the definitions for the word in dark type in each sentence. Then, see which sentence makes sense. Don't be tricked by a different meaning of the same word.

1. a gift
   a. At **present**, we are still required to attend class.
   b. The best birthday **present** Janice received was her driver's license!

2. to send off
   a. The guests were taken to the ship by a motor **launch**.
   b. Some people feel that the weather was too cold to **launch** the Challenger into space.

3. a covered container for water
   a. Most army posts have a **canteen** for the soldiers.
   b. A **canteen** is essential for traveling in the desert.

4. something unusual
   a. His **curiosity** tempted him to ask her if she had ever skated before.
   b. The movie *Mask* was about a boy whose physical deformity made him a **curiosity** at school.

5. unable to be reached
   a. Some school principals are **inaccessible** to the student body.
   b. For centuries, Mount Everest was **inaccessible** to climbers.

6. simplicity
   a. Her **innocence** was proven when the evidence was submitted to the jury.
   b. His **innocence** and humility impressed the teacher.

7. spreading out of control
   a. The **raging** trainer was arrested before the bear was hurt.
   b. It is difficult to contain a **raging** fire in populated areas.

8. prefer something
   a. Only after we changed the flat tire and got her car started, did she **favor** us with a smile.
   b. Many Americans **favor** chocolate ice cream over apple pie.

Word Parts

In Part 4, you are going to learn another method for guessing what a new word means. You will learn to look at parts of an unfamiliar word to see if the parts can give you a clue to the word's overall meaning. Sometimes a part of a new word will be a word you already know. Sometimes a word has special parts added at the beginning or end—a prefix or a suffix. You will learn to use these word parts as meaning clues.

Look at the two pictures below. One picture illustrates the meaning of the word **distraught**. The other illustrates the meaning of the word **composed**. Can you match each picture with the right word? On your paper, write your guess about each word's meaning.

Sometimes you will see an unfamiliar word in your reading or on a vocabulary test. You may notice that you can spot a word you already know within the new word. Many times, you can use the word inside, called the *base word*, to help you determine what the new word means. This trick does not always work, but it can sometimes help.

Another way to use word parts as clues is to look at a prefix or suffix added to a base word. Knowing the meaning of a prefix or suffix can help you figure out the overall meaning of a new word.

Here are a few prefixes and suffixes and their meanings.

PREFIXES
inter- (between)
con- (together)
dis- (do the opposite of)
heter- (other than)
re- (back)

SUFFIXES
-ness (noun form of word)
-able (able)
-mania (insanity)
-less (not having)
-ory (place of)

Read the following story about art deco. Three words are printed in dark type. Use the base words and other word parts to help you guess the meaning of the new words.

In 1925, an exposition of arts was held in Paris. It was called "The Exposition **International** des Arts Decoratifs et Industrials Modernes," and from this came the term "art deco." It imitates the decorative style of the 1920's and 1930's. It includes a **heterogeneous** group of objects, lamps, utensils, mirrors, and book illustrations which are characterized by bold outlines, streamlined forms, and the use of plastic materials. San Francisco is the present home of **decomania**.

1. The prefix *inter-* and the base word **national** help you guess that **international** means __.
   a. between nations   b. without nations

2. The prefix *heter-* helps you guess that **heterogeneous** means __.
   a. similar   b. dissimilar

3. The suffix *-mania* helps you guess that **decomania** means __.
   a. mad about art deco   b. wise about decorating

Check your answers. You should have picked **a** for 1, **b** for 2, and **a** for 3.

139

A. Look at the words in List 1 below. Try to find a base word you already know inside each new word. Notice any prefixes or suffixes. Match each new word with its meaning in List 2.

LIST 1
1. heterodox
2. malcontent
3. disorder
4. bilingual
5. conservatory

LIST 2
a. one who is not satisfied
b. confusion
c. different from the standard
d. house for growing plants
e. speaking two languages

Check your answers. You should have chosen **c** for 1, **a** for 2, **b** for 3, **e** for 4, and **d** for 5.

B. Read the following paragraph about another art form. Look for the word parts to help you define the words in dark type. Then, answer the questions on page 141. Put your answers on your paper.

We tend to **disassociate** sewing from pure art, but one of the newest developments in modern art **necessitates** a **capability** with needle and thread. This is the creation of the free flowing, colorful, and **multishaped** forms made from silk or gauzy fabric. They float like giant kites or butterflies between city buildings—or pause, suspended in the air, over gardens where busy workers and shoppers are **recreating** before returning to their offices or homes.

1. Which word means *refreshing*?
2. Which word means to *separate in the mind*?
3. Which word means *requires*?
4. Which word means *having many shapes*?
5. Which word means *skill*?

Check your answers. Your answers should be 1. recreating, 2. disassociate, 3. necessitates, 4. multishaped, 5. capability.

C. Here are the kinds of questions you sometimes see on reading tests. Read each incomplete sentence. Then, find the answer that best completes the sentence. Look for base words and other word parts to help you choose your answers. Put your answers on your paper.

1. When you **negate** an idea you __.
   a. choose it
   b. deny it
   c. desire it

2. When you **protract** an argument, you __.
   a. break it up
   b. prolong it
   c. avoid it

3. When you **requite** a person for aid received, you __.
   a. repay him
   b. ignore him
   c. praise him

4. A **trackless** trolley would be powered by __.
   a. an engine or overhead power
   b. tracks
   c. the road itself

5. A person with a **waspish** disposition is __.
   a. mean and sharp-tongued
   b. sweet and kind
   c. pleasant but thoughtless

Check your answers. You should have picked **b** for 1, **b** for 2, **a** for 3, **a** for 4, and **a** for 5.

Here are the eight new words in this lesson. Their meanings are not listed. Notice how the words are used in the passage. Also, pay close attention to base words, prefixes, and suffixes. They will help you define the new words.

discount   permeating
incontestable   relax
musicologists   perceptible
minimize   impressionable

Music Power

Aristotle said long ago that most of the learning that influences us comes in through our ears. Once the printing press was invented in the 15th century, and people began to read, experts tended to **discount** Aristotle's idea. Today, however, some scientists think he may have been on to something. Certainly the music that is heard, even when the listener is not conscious of listening, seems to have an **incontestable** influence on attitudes and behavior.

Take *Muzak,* for example. Muzak is a very profitable company run by **musicologists** who sell music programs that reach 80 million people a day in 17 countries. They have discovered that workers reach a low productivity level in the middle of the morning and again in the middle of the afternoon. Therefore, they provide stimulating music at those times. At other times, they present more relaxing music to lessen tensions and **minimize** conflicts. Merchants have found that sedate music **permeating** supermarkets causes customers to shop more slowly and thus find more things they want to buy.

In hospitals, music can lower blood pressure, help ease headaches, and regulate irregular heartbeats. In mental hospitals, music helps patients **relax** and focus on the real world.

Why music has so much power is the subject of an ongoing study. Dr. Lee Salk believes that the baby in the womb is comforted by the rhythm of the mother's heartbeat. Then when the baby is an infant being carried around, she usually carries the child on her left side, near the *aorta,* which is normally the source of the **perceptible** heartbeat.

Some people are far more **impressionable** than others. There are people who can have an epileptic seizure upon hearing music. The important point to remember is that music has the power to influence mental and physical activity. It makes sense to listen with an open ear to what we hear and to listen selectively.

A. Look for word parts in the lesson words to help you pick the best meanings in the questions below. Write your answers on your paper.

1. The prefix and base word of **discount** help you know it means to reduce the value or __.
   a. disregard
   b. count more
   c. not count at all

2. The prefix *in-* means *not.* You know what *contest* means, so **incontestable** means __.
   a. questionable
   b. doubtful
   c. cannot be questioned

3. The suffix *-ology* means *study of,* so you can guess that a **musicologist** is __.
   a. a music lover
   b. one who studies music
   c. a band leader

4. The prefix *mini-* helps you know that **minimize** means __.
   a. make little
   b. make more
   c. make enough

5. The prefix *per-* means *through.* This helps you know that **permeating** means __.
   a. going under
   b. going over
   c. going through

6. The prefix *re-* means *back* and *lax* means *to loosen.* This helps you know that to **relax** is __.
   a. to become less stiff
   b. to tighten up
   c. to cut class

7. Perceptible has the same prefix as *permeate.* It means __.
   a. capable of being detected
   b. cannot be visible
   c. barely or almost seen

8. You know the words *impress* and *impression.* **Impressionable** must mean __.
   a. easily seen
   b. easily heard
   c. easily influenced

B. Write a sentence to answer each question below. Use the lesson word in dark type in your sentence.

1. When you want to **relax**, what kind of music do you like to hear?
2. What **incontestable** evidence is there that music affects people?
3. Who do you think is a very **impressionable** musician?

Here are the eight new words in this lesson. Their meanings are not listed. Notice how the words are used in the passage. Also, pay close attention to base words, prefixes, and suffixes. They will help you define the new words.

provoke	**vulgarism**
revered	**remnants**
insensitive	**extraordinary**
bicentennial	**conspicuous**

Trashy Art

Modern art, like modern music, is always seeking new expressions that **provoke** thought and challenge technique. Some experts claim this is self-expression. Others feel that it is an attempt to grab the public's attention and force them to think about issues. Still others say that art is its own reason for existence. Take it as it strikes you.

For example, there is a water symphony made by recording a leaky faucet and then electronically varying the speed of the drips. And in Boston, our **revered** "cradle of the American Revolution and home of great patriots," is a display of art made from trash.

In Haymarket Square, one can see curious visitors gingerly stepping over shiny cabbage leaves, bean pods, crushed egg cartons, smashed pizza crust, crumpled newspaper, corn husks, and pop rings from beer cans. Rats and flies don't feast on this creation because the garbage is cast in bronze and set in concrete. Believe it or not, this is no **insensitive** joke. It is a serious work of art, commissioned by the city of Boston during its **bicentennial** celebration. The work is called *Asaroton 1976*, meaning "unswept floor."

This display is not a **vulgarism** created as a reaction to a garbage strike, but is inspired, rather, by the mosaic on the floor of an ancient Roman home. The mosaic showed the **remnants** of a feast. The *Asaroton 1976* seems to be a rebellion against so many monuments which reflect Boston's historical settings — the Freedom Trail, the Tea Party Boat, Old Ironsides, and Paul Revere's Old North Church.

Perhaps all this is a bronze warning not to take ourselves too seriously. Maybe, such a work of art is a celebration of the common man, of the heroism of ordinary people who live and work in large cities. At any rate, *Asaroton 1976* is modern and **extraordinary** enough to be in Los Angeles or in San Francisco. But in either place, it might be barely noticeable. In Boston, at least, it is **conspicuous**.

A. Look for word parts in the lesson words to help you pick the best meanings in the questions below. Write your answers on your paper.

1. The word **provoke** means to stimulate. In combination with "thought" it means __.
   a. thought-stopping
   b. causing thought
   c. to confuse

2. The word **revered** has the same base as *reverend*. This should help you guess that **revered** means __.
   a. honored
   b. disgraced
   c. renowned

3. The prefix *in-* and the base word *sense* help you know that **insensitive** means __.
   a. sensible
   b. not caring
   c. unseen

4. The prefix *bi-* means *two*. Boston was celebrating its **bicentennial** or __ year.
   a. 200th
   b. 100th
   c. 300th

5. If you know what the word *vulgar* means, you know a **vulgarism** is __.
   a. a coarse remark or work
   b. a noble word or work
   c. an unusual word or work

6. The word *remains* has the same base as **remnants**. This helps you know **remnants** means parts that are __.
   a. dirty
   b. unwanted
   c. leftovers

7. **Extraordinary** is made from two words and means __.
   a. something common
   b. something different
   c. something psychic

8. The base of **conspicuous** gives us the word *spy*. This helps you guess that **conspicuous** means __.
   a. illegal
   b. invisible
   c. visible

B. Write a sentence to answer each question below. Use the lesson word in dark type in your sentence.

1. What is the most **extraordinary** thing that has ever happened to you?
2. In what year did America celebrate its **bicentennial**?
3. Name a historical figure who is **revered**, but doesn't deserve to be.

TAKING TESTS

Choose the word or phrase that best completes each sentence. Put your answers on your answer sheet.

Test Tips: This kind of question asks you to think about the meaning of the key word. Then, you need to use that meaning to choose the best answer. Read the incomplete sentence carefully. Use word parts to help you guess the meaning of each key word.

---

1. If a student provokes a teacher, he or she ___.
   a. pleases the teacher
   b. questions the teacher
   c. replies to the teacher
   d. makes the teacher angry

2. To minimize problems with your teacher regarding your unfinished assignment, say ___.
   a. "I'll get to it next year."
   b. "The ten-page paper will be ready tomorrow."
   c. "I have more important things to do."
   d. "I don't have to do it."

3. A judge who discounts the testimony of a witness ___.
   a. accepts it
   b. questions it
   c. disregards it
   d. criticizes it

4. An impressionable freshman is likely to believe that ___.
   a. classes start on time
   b. assignments are due regularly
   c. joining clubs is a good way to make friends
   d. seniors are to be feared

5. If remnants of food are left out on the table, they ___.
   a. taste great   c. turn gray
   b. draw bugs   d. get stolen

6. An incontestable evidence that you were not at the beach on Friday would be ___.
   a. a note from the lifeguard
   b. a note from your mother
   c. a recorded phone call to school from your best friend
   d. your presence in class at the time

7. An extraordinary event in school might be when ___.
   a. Mr. Dozingoff retires after 60 years as principal
   b. the teacher expects finished assignments on time
   c. classes are cancelled because of a storm
   d. a senior tells a freshman that the auditorium is haunted

8. Vulgarisms tend to make speech sound ___.
   a. interesting and exciting
   b. coarse and crude
   c. clever and witty
   d. loud and clear

UNIT III
STUDY SKILLS

PART 1

Visual Materials

You can get facts in many different ways:

A. By reading a passage.

The 1985 report of the U.S. Census Bureau shows that about 51% of the U.S. population are females and about a quarter of the population are between ages 35 and 59 years old. A little more than a third are 20 to 34 years old, and one fifth are under 20 years of age.

The report also shows that about 26% of the population live in the rural areas and 74% live in the cities.

B. By looking at maps. (Maps are drawings of parts of the world.)

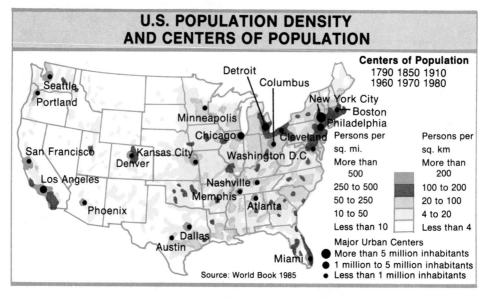

U.S. POPULATION DENSITY AND CENTERS OF POPULATION

Source: World Book 1985

C. By reading a chart called a table. (A table is a list of facts.)

U.S. POPULATION 1880-1985

Census Year	Population	Census Year	Population
1880	50,155,783	1940	131,669,275
1890	62,974,714	1950	150,669,361
1900	75,994,575	1960	179,323,175
1910	91,972,266	1970	203,235,298
1920	105,710,620	1980	226,545,805
1930	122,775,046	1985	237,291,121

D. By looking at a graph where the facts really stand out.

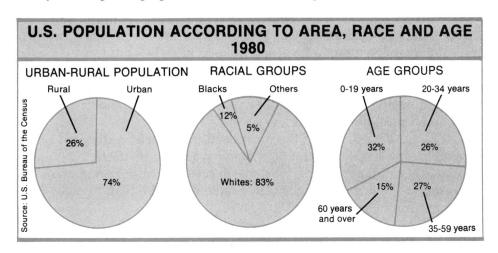

U.S. POPULATION ACCORDING TO AREA, RACE AND AGE 1980

URBAN-RURAL POPULATION   RACIAL GROUPS   AGE GROUPS

Source: U.S. Bureau of the Census

Read the questions below. They are based on the visual materials you just studied. Write the correct answers on your paper.

1. Which visual material best shows the U.S. population by age groups?

   a. graph   c. table
   b. map   d. passage

2. Which visual material shows that most of the U.S. residents are in the eastern half of the country?

   a. passage   c. table
   b. map   d. graph

3. Which visual material best shows how the population has increased over a 100-year period?

   a. passage   c. table
   b. map   d. graph

4. Which visual material best shows the population distribution by urban/rural, racial, and age groups?

   a. passage   c. table
   b. map   d. graph

City of Romance

Paris, France, has been the world's idea of a beautiful and romantic city for hundreds of years. It was founded 52 years before Christ was born, and every generation has tried to keep Paris beautiful.

At the time of the Crusades, Prince Philip II decided to make Paris the center of culture, learning and beauty. Later kings ordered the building of palaces and wide boulevards. Napoleon demanded more gardens and public buildings.

The *Champs Elysees*, one of the most beautiful streets in the world, was built in the 1700's and the *Eiffel Tower* was built in 1899.

Today's generation is doing its share in restoring, preserving and enhancing the beauty of the city. They have devised a plan to make it a more beautiful Paris by year 2000.

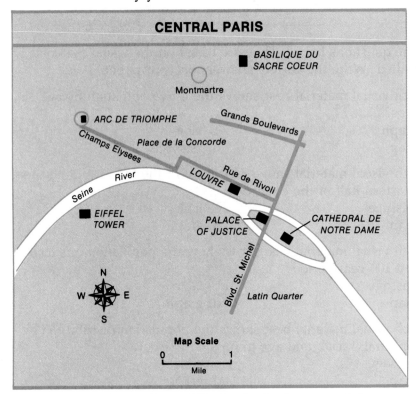

The map above shows Central Paris. At the bottom of the map are a map scale and compass rose.

150

Use the map on page 150 to answer these questions.

1. The *Seine River* divides Paris into the right bank in the north and the left bank in the south. Where is *Place de la Concorde?*
   a. left bank, center of the city
   b. right bank, center of the city
   c. right bank, east of the city
   d. not inside the city

Check your answer. Find the *Seine River* on the map. Find the *Place de la Concorde.* It is north of the river in the center of the city. The answer is **b**.

2. About how far is the *Eiffel Tower* from the *Arc de Triomphe?*
   a. 3 miles
   b. 5 miles
   c. 9 miles
   d. 1.5 miles

3. *Montmartre*, a beautiful hill above the city, is famous for its artists who have painted there since the nineteenth century. *The Basilique du Sacre Coeur*, a huge white church is __ of *Montmartre.*
   a. northeast
   b. southeast
   c. south
   d. east

4. Central Paris is about __ wide.
   a. 6 miles
   b. 2 miles
   c. 10 miles
   d. 18 miles

5. The *Seine River* is about 480 miles long. About __ of the river flows through the city.
   a. 10 miles
   b. 14 miles
   c. 3 miles
   d. 7 miles

6. The most famous art museum in the world is the *Louvre.* About how far is it from the *Cathedral de Notre Dame*, a church famous for its stained glass windows?
   a. 2 miles
   b. 1 mile
   c. 8 miles
   d. 5 miles

7. What road would you take to get from the *Palace of Justice* to the *Latin Quarter?*
   a. *Boulevard St. Michel*, south
   b. *Grands Boulevards*, west
   c. *Champs Elysees*, north
   d. *Rue de Rivoli*, east

8. To get to the *Arc de Triomphe* from the *Place de la Concorde*, you would travel __.
   a. south on *Rue de Rivoli*
   b. northwest on *Champs Elysees*
   c. south on *Boulevard St. Michel*
   d. west on *Grands Boulevards*

U.S. Money Manager

The word *bank* comes from the Italian word *banca*, meaning "bench" or "counter" on which to display money.

In America, banks issued their own money until 1936. The banks then did not always have enough gold to back up the paper money. So, the Federal Reserve System was established, as an independent agency of the government, to direct the nation's banking system and manage the nation's supply of money. It is directed by seven administrators, each appointed by the President for a 14-year term. The Federal Reserve System provides many financial services to the country's commercial banks as well as to the federal government.

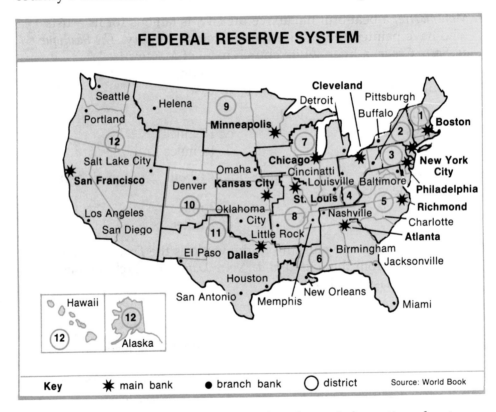

FEDERAL RESERVE SYSTEM

Key ✳ main bank ● branch bank ◯ district   Source: World Book

A special-purpose map is any map that shows information about one specialized subject. The special-purpose map above shows the main and branch banks under the Federal Reserve System as they are spread out all over the United States.

Use the map and its key on page 152 to answer these questions. Choose the best answer.

1. How many Federal Reserve districts are there?
a. 4
b. 7
c. 12
d. 50

Check your answer. There are 12 districts marked on the map. The answer is **c**.

2. The northeast is serviced by __ bank districts.
a. 3
b. 7
c. 2
d. 6

3. On the west coast, the main Federal Reserve Bank of California is in __.
a. Los Angeles
b. San Diego
c. Oakland
d. San Francisco

4. A Federal Reserve System main bank is in __, Texas.
a. Dallas
b. Houston
c. San Antonio
d. El Paso

5. A Federal Reserve note with the number 1 on it would indicate it was issued by a district bank in __.
a. Salt Lake City
b. Boston
c. Kansas City
d. New York City

6. Which Federal Reserve district covers the greatest territory?
a. District 11
b. District 10
c. District 6
d. District 12

7. How many Federal Reserve branch banks are there?
a. 25
b. 15
c. 12
d. 32

8. The greatest number of main Federal Reserve banks is __.
a. on the east coast
b. in the south
c. on the west coast
d. in the midwest

LESSON 3

A Natural Wonder

The Grand Canyon, formed over millions of years by the Colorado River as it flows through Arizona, is one of the Seven Natural Wonders of the World. This giant *gorge* (deep narrow pass between heights) is 217 miles long and over a mile deep. The first European to view it was Garcia Lopez de Cardenas in 1540, and the first boat trip through the rapids was conducted by John Powell in 1869.

The Grand Canyon is sliced through with gorgeous rock formations of every color, and is the outstanding beauty in a state of beautiful deserts, mountains and scenic wonders. Each year two million people come from all over the world, many of whom travel the narrow trails by mule, to gaze in wonder at the Grand Canyon's magnificence.

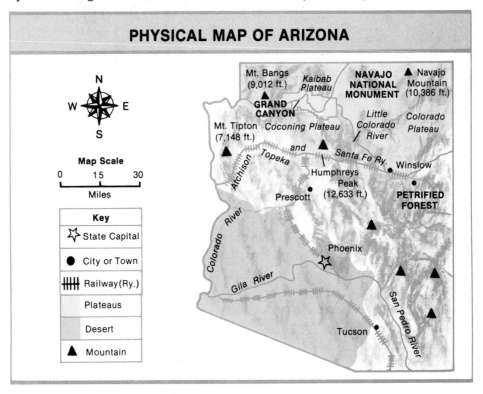

PHYSICAL MAP OF ARIZONA

Street and road maps show direction and the routes of state, interstate and local roads. On a physical map, the mountains, hills, deserts, rivers and plateaus are featured.

154

Use the map and its key on page 154 to answer these questions. Choose the best answer.

1. Where in Arizona is the Grand Canyon?
a. in the north   c. west of Mt. Bangs
b. southeast of Phoenix   d. in the center of the state

Check your answer. Find the Grand Canyon. It is neither near Phoenix nor is it west of Mt. Bangs. The answer is **a**.

2. Around the Grand Canyon are __.
a. deserts   c. valleys
b. mountain regions   d. plateaus

3. The capital of Arizona is __.
a. Prescott   c. Tucson
b. Phoenix   d. Winslow

4. The Petrified Forest is __ of the Grand Canyon.
a. northeast   c. southwest
b. west   d. southeast

5. The highest point of elevation in Arizona is __.
a. Mt. Tipton   c. Navajo Mountain
b. Mt. Bangs   d. Humphreys Peak

6. Flowing southeast from the Grand Canyon is __.
a. the Little Colorado   c. the Colorado River
b. the Gila River   d. the San Pedro River

7. The Navajo National Monument is __.
a. south of the Grand Canyon
b. at the base of a mountain
c. on the Little Colorado River
d. all of the above

8. Transportation routes on physical maps are __.
a. roads and airports   c. airports and railways
b. rivers and railways   d. roads and bus routes

Wealth in the Poorest Continent

Africa is the second largest continent on earth. It has 51 independent countries and 545 million people. However, 50 of these countries are classified as economically undeveloped. Yet there is great wealth there, buried under the surface of the earth.

South Africa is the largest producer of gold and diamonds in the world. There are also gold and diamonds in the central and western parts of Africa. Most of the world's platinum is mined in Africa. Oil, copper, uranium, and other minerals are plentiful on the continent.

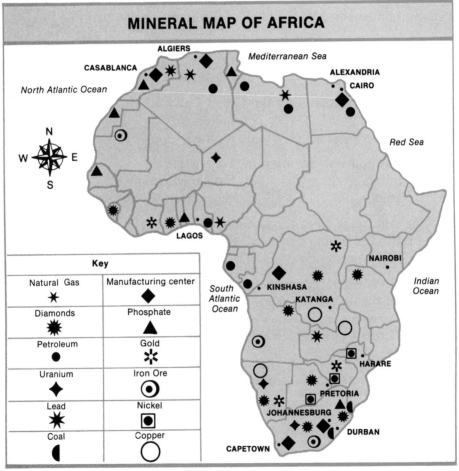

MINERAL MAP OF AFRICA

The product map above shows where some of the minerals in Africa are mined and manufactured. Study the map, its compass rose and key.

Use the map on page 156 to answer these questions. Choose the best answer.

1. According to the map, there are __ diamond mines in Africa.
   a. 12   c. 9
   b. 5   d. 18

Check your answer. Find the symbol for diamond on the map key. Count the symbols on the map. The answer is **c**.

2. According to the map, how many major manufacturing centers are there on this huge continent?
   a. 6   c. 12
   b. 60   d. 10

3. Which part of Africa seems to have no minerals?
   a. west Africa   c. south Africa
   b. central Africa   d. northeast Africa

4. Where is most of Africa's petroleum found?
   a. in the north   c. on the east coast
   b. south of the diamond mines   d. west of the gold mines

5. Where are the largest deposits of diamonds found?
   a. in central Africa   c. primarily in the south
   b. only in South Africa   d. along the coastline

6. Along which coast are there more phosphates?
   a. North Atlantic Ocean
   b. South Atlantic Ocean
   c. Indian Ocean
   d. Red Sea

7. Which mineral is not mined in Africa?
   a. diamonds   c. emeralds
   b. gold   d. petroleum

8. According to the map, Africa mines __.
   a. more uranium than gold   c. more uranium than nickel
   b. as much copper as nickel   d. more gold than diamonds

The Bowl Games

During the winter holidays, Americans are hooked on the bowl games — cheering outside the stadium or in front of a TV set. More than 700 colleges and universities sponsor football games. Most of these belong to athletic conferences, leagues or associations which make the rules and supervise the competitions.

Most college teams play 11 games a season. At the end of the season, the best teams are invited to play in the bowl games.

The professional leagues choose their players from among outstanding college players through a selection system known as the "draft." These professional teams generally play 16 games and the winning teams in the playoffs go to the Super Bowl.

MAJOR COLLEGIATE BOWL GAMES

Game	Location	Year Started
Aloha Bowl	Honolulu, Hawaii	1982
Bluebonnet Bowl	Houston, Tex.	1959
California Bowl	Fresno, Calif.	1981
Cherry Bowl	Pontiac, Mich.	1984
Cotton Bowl	Dallas, Tex.	1937
Fiesta Bowl	Tempe, Ariz.	1971
Florida Citrus Bowl	Orlando, Fla.	1947
Freedom Bowl	Anaheim, Calif.	1984
Gator Bowl	Jacksonville, Fla.	1946
Hall of Fame Classic	Birmingham, Ala.	1977
Holiday Bowl	San Diego, Calif.	1978
Independence Bowl	Shreveport, La.	1978
Liberty Bowl	Memphis, Tenn.	1959
Orange Bowl	Miami, Fla.	1933
Peach Bowl	Atlanta, Ga.	1968
Rose Bowl	Pasadena, Calif.	1902
Sugar Bowl	New Orleans, La.	1935
Sun Bowl	El Paso, Tex.	1936

SUPER BOWL

1967 Green Bay Packers (NFL) 35, Kansas City Chiefs (AFL) 10
1968 Green Bay Packers (NFL) 33, Oakland Raiders (AFL) 14
1969 New York Jets (AFL) 16, Baltimore Colts (NFL) 7
1970 Kansas City Chiefs (AFL) 23, Minnesota Vikings (NFL) 7
1971 Baltimore Colts (AFC) 16, Dallas Cowboys (NFC) 13
1972 Dallas Cowboys (NFC) 24, Miami Dolphins (AFC) 3
1973 Miami Dolphins (AFC) 14, Washington Redskins (NFC) 7
1974 Miami Dolphins (AFC) 24, Minnesota Vikings (NFC) 7
1975 Pittsburgh Steelers (AFC) 16, Minnesota Vikings (NFC) 6
1976 Pittsburgh Steelers (AFC) 21, Dallas Cowboys (NFC) 17
1977 Oakland Raiders (AFC) 32, Minnesota Vikings (NFC) 14
1978 Dallas Cowboys (NFC) 27, Denver Broncos (AFC) 10
1979 Pittsburgh Steelers (AFC) 35, Dallas Cowboys (NFC) 31
1980 Pittsburgh Steelers (AFC) 31, Los Angeles Rams (NFC) 19
1981 Oakland Raiders (AFC) 27, Philadelphia Eagles (NFC) 10
1982 San Francisco 49ers (NFC) 26, Cincinnati Bengals (AFC) 21
1983 Washington Redskins (NFC) 27, Miami Dolphins (AFC) 17
1984 Los Angeles Raiders (AFC) 38, Washington Redskins (NFC) 9
1985 San Francisco 49ers (NFC) 38, Miami Dolphins (AFC) 16
1986 Chicago Bears (AFC) 46, New England Patriots (NFC) 10
1987 New York Giants (NFC) 39, Denver Broncos (AFC) 20

A table is arranged in columns and rows. A column is read from top to bottom. A row is read from left to right. In the first table above, find the name of the collegiate bowl and read across the line to learn where and when it started. In the second table, find the year and read across the line to learn which teams played in the Super Bowl.

158

Use the tables on page 158 to answer these questions. Choose the best answer.

1. In what year did the Orange Bowl open?
   a. 1933   c. 1936
   b. 1968   d. 1902

Check your answer. Find the Orange Bowl on the Major Collegiate Bowl Games table. Read across to the date. The answer is **a**.

2. What was the first collegiate bowl game played?
   a. Orange Bowl   c. Cotton Bowl
   b. Rose Bowl   d. Sugar Bowl

3. Where is the Sugar Bowl played?
   a. in Pasadena, California   c. in Dallas, Texas
   b. in New Orleans, Louisiana   d. in a sugar field

4. Which state sponsors the most bowl games each year?
   a. California   c. Louisiana
   b. Florida   d. Texas

5. Which professional team has won the most Super Bowl games?
   a. Green Bay Packers   c. Pittsburgh Steelers
   b. Oakland Raiders   d. Chicago Bears

6. Which team has lost the most Super Bowl games?
   a. Minnesota Vikings   c. Denver Broncos
   b. Miami Dolphins   d. Dallas Cowboys

7. In which Super Bowl year did a team win with the most point-spread?
   a. 1986   c. 1981
   b. 1984   d. 1977

8. The state which sponsored a most recently organized collegiate bowl game is ___.
   a. Hawaii   c. New Jersey
   b. Kansas   d. California

LESSON 6

Be a Robot Repairperson

At the beginning of the American Revolution, the battle cry was "The British are coming!" Today, the cry of the technological revolution is "The robots are coming!" Many workers see these developments in robotics (science of robots) as an attack on their jobs. Manufacturers see it as an inevitable step in more efficient production to compete with the rest of the manufacturing countries.

Robots are here to stay and they are getting cheaper to produce. They are being used in a variety of ways — assembling, welding, painting and material handling. It looks as if a good field to train for would be in the manufacture and repair of robots.

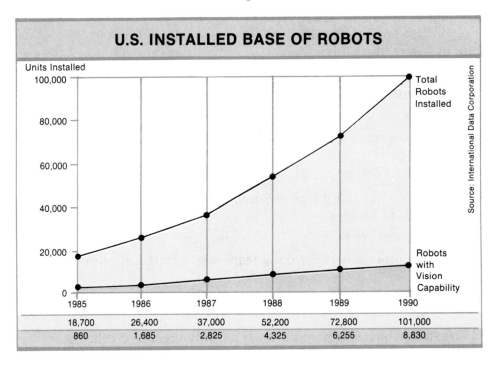

U.S. INSTALLED BASE OF ROBOTS

Source: International Data Corporation

	1985	1986	1987	1988	1989	1990
Total Robots Installed	18,700	26,400	37,000	52,200	72,800	101,000
Robots with Vision Capability	860	1,685	2,825	4,325	6,255	8,830

The line graph above shows the increasing number of robots installed and used in the U.S. The numbers on the left side show the total units already installed. The dates across the bottom show the years in which they were installed or expect to be installed. The top line shows the total number of robots. The bottom line shows the number of robots with vision capability.

Use the graph on page 160 to answer these questions. Choose the best answer.

1. About how many robots in all were in use in 1985?
   a. none
   b. 18,000
   c. 800
   d. 23,000

Check your answer. Find 1985 on the graph. Read up to the dot just below 20,000. The answer is **b**.

2. About how many robots in all will be in use by 1990?
   a. 18,000
   b. 100,000
   c. 52,000
   d. 10,000

3. About how many robots with vision capability were in use in 1986?
   a. 100
   b. 2,000
   c. 15,000
   d. 30,000

4. Which year projects the greatest number of installed robots?
   a. 1985
   b. 1986
   c. 1987
   d. 1990

5. By 1990, how many robots with vision capability will be installed?
   a. 10,000
   b. less than 10,000
   c. more than 10,000
   d. 100,000

6. How many robots without vision capability were in use in 1985?
   a. 860
   b. 18,700
   c. 19,560
   d. 17,840

7. The graph indicates that the installation of robots __.
   a. decreased in 1986
   b. increased in 1985
   c. is on the decline
   d. is rapidly increasing

8. In 1989, the total number of robots with vision capability will be __ than in 1988.
   a. 6,255 more
   b. 6,255 less
   c. 1,930 more
   d. 1,930 less

Crowded Cities

By the year 2000, half of the world's population will be crowding the cities. Mexico City, already the world's most populated city with over 18 million people, is expected to have over 26 million people in the year 2000. Sao Paulo, Brazil will have 24 million, and Calcutta and Bombay in India about 16 million people living in each city.

The government officials of overcrowded cities are working together to find and plan ways of meeting the demands for water, transportation, employment, housing and sanitation that these cities will require.

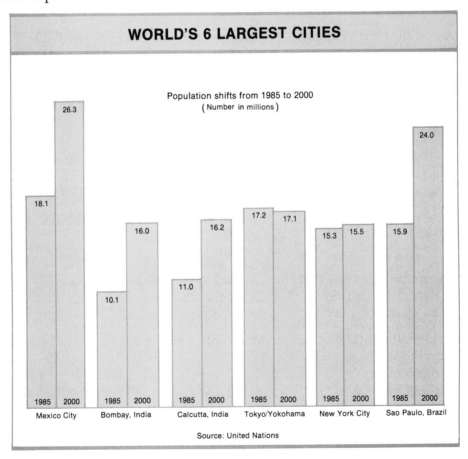

WORLD'S 6 LARGEST CITIES

Population shifts from 1985 to 2000
(Number in millions)

Source: United Nations

This bar graph shows the world's largest cities and their projected population growth.

Use the graph on page 162 to answer these questions. Choose the best answer.

1. In 1985, the second most populated city in the world was __.
   a. Mexico City   c. Tokyo/Yokohama
   b. New York City   d. Bombay

Check your answer. Check each graph for 1985. The bar for the second largest number represents Tokyo/Yokohama. The answer is **c.**

2. By the year 2000, what will be the most populated city in the world?
   a. Mexico City   c. New York City
   b. Sao Paulo   d. Calcutta

3. Which country has two of the most overcrowded cities in the world?
   a. India   c. Japan
   b. Mexico   d. Brazil

4. Which city expects little growth in population within the fifteen-year period?
   a. Sao Paulo   c. Tokyo/Yokohama
   b. New York City   d. Calcutta

5. By the year 2000, how many more people will live in the Tokyo/Yokohama area in Japan than in New York City?
   a. 1.6 million   c. 2.1 million
   b. 2 million   d. .5 million

6. How many people in all will Bombay and Calcutta have by the year 2000?
   a. 30 million   c. 21.1 million
   b. 32 million   d. 27.2 million

7. How many more people does New York City expect to have in year 2000?
   a. 1 million   c. .5 million
   b. .2 million   d. 1.5 million

8. What urban area expects a decrease in population by the year 2000?
   a. Sao Paulo   c. Mexico City
   b. Calcutta   d. Tokyo/Yokohama

LESSON 8

Here Come the Brides (And Grooms)!

Some say that marriage has gone out of style, and that most people are single or divorced. But the statistics show that most of the U.S. population still prefer to say "I do (want to live with you — till death do us part)" and make it happen, if they can.

The problems of dating, courtship, and marriage get more publicity today, and that may be good in many ways. People think about the problems they will face, and try to solve them together. They try harder to be considerate and helpful to their partners. Today, men try to share the burdens of housework and child-bearing, and women try to assume the responsibility of contributing to the family income.

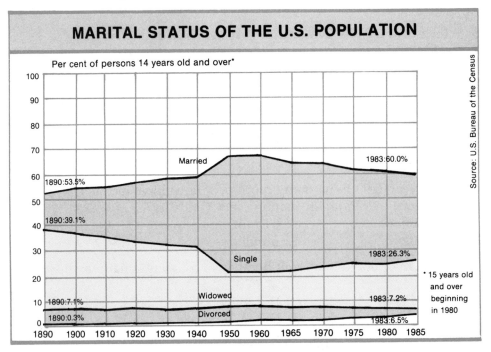

The complex line graph uses lines of different lengths to compare quantities. The graph above compares people of different legal status over a period of 93 years. The key tells you what status each line represents. To read the graph, look at where each line ends. Then follow the lines on the graph to the left. The number at the end of the line tells you the percentage of persons 14 years and older in that group.

164

Use the graph on page 164 to answer these questions. Choose the best answer.

1. How much has the percentage of married people increased since 1890?
   a. 8%   c. 10%
   b. 6.5%   d. 12%

Check your answer. The percentage of married people in 1890 is 53.5. Subtract that from the percentage for 1983. The answer is **b**.

2. How much has the percentage of the single population decreased since 1890?
   a. 12.8%   c. 8.9%
   b. 10%   d. 30%

3. How much has the divorce rate increased from 1900 to 1983?
   a. 3.2%   c. 5.8%
   b. 6.2%   d. 10%

4. In which year was the percentage of the married population above 67%?
   a. 1983   c. 1940
   b. 1960   d. 1965

5. Between which years did the marriage rate peak and the single rate decline?
   a. 1940 to 1950   c. 1930 to 1940
   b. 1910 to 1930   d. 1890 to 1910

6. The __ statuses have remained stable between 1960 and 1970.
   a. married and widowed   c. married and divorced
   b. divorced and unmarried   d. widowed and divorced

7. Which group shows the greatest change over the years?
   a. married people   c. divorced people
   b. single people   d. widows and widowers

8. The graph shows that only the __ status has steadily increased though the years.
   a. single   c. widowed
   b. divorced   d. married

Air Pollutants

Air pollution is a modern problem that has gained widespread public concern. An update on the quality of the air we breathe is now part of the regular T.V. report every evening.

Many different things cause the air quality to vary from day to day. The pollutants themselves vary in each area. Cloud cover, moisture content, wind and weather conditions hold the pollutants down or move them around and scatter them.

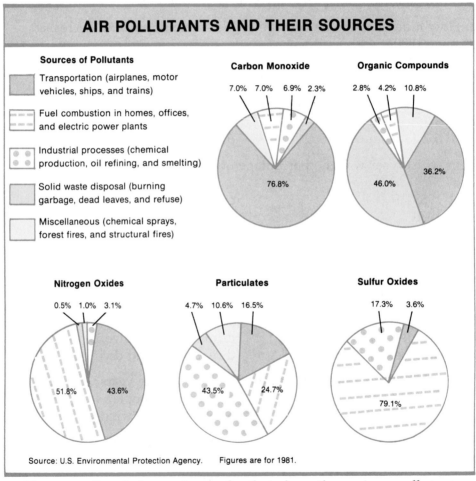

AIR POLLUTANTS AND THEIR SOURCES

Sources of Pollutants

Transportation (airplanes, motor vehicles, ships, and trains)

Fuel combustion in homes, offices, and electric power plants

Industrial processes (chemical production, oil refining, and smelting)

Solid waste disposal (burning garbage, dead leaves, and refuse)

Miscellaneous (chemical sprays, forest fires, and structural fires)

Carbon Monoxide
7.0% 7.0% 6.9% 2.3%
76.8%

Organic Compounds
2.8% 4.2% 10.8%
36.2%
46.0%

Nitrogen Oxides
0.5% 1.0% 3.1%
51.8% 43.6%

Particulates
4.7% 10.6% 16.5%
43.5% 24.7%

Sulfur Oxides
17.3% 3.6%
79.1%

Source: U.S. Environmental Protection Agency.   Figures are for 1981.

Above are five circle or pie graphs that show the various pollutants. Most of these are caused by artificially created wastes in the form of gases and small particles of liquid and solid matter.

Use the circle graphs and key on page 166 to answer these questions. Choose the correct answer.

1. What is the primary cause of carbon monoxide in the atmosphere?
   a. power plants   c. fires
   b. transportation   d. waste disposal

Check your answer. Find the circle graph for carbon monoxide. Use the key to learn what the largest area of circle represents. The answer is **b**.

2. Nitrogen oxides come from __ and fuel combustion.
   a. fires   c. transportation
   b. industry   d. waste disposal

3. Particulates in the air come primarily from __.
   a. industry   c. fires
   b. transportation   d. chemical sprays

4. Sulfur oxides come primarily from __.
   a. transportation   c. solid waste disposal
   b. fuel combustion   d. forest fires

5. Almost half of polluting organic compounds come from __.
   a. solid waste disposal c. forest fires
   b. industrial processes d. transportation

6. Transportation and __ are the primary sources of polluting gases and particles in the air.
   a. fuel combustion   c. solid waste disposal
   b. industrial processes d. chemical sprays

7. The least source of pollution, but nevertheless a source, is __.
   a. forest fires   c. oil refining
   b. transportation   d. solid waste disposal

8. Carbon monoxide comes from more sources than __.
   a. particulates   c. organic compounds
   b. nitrogen oxide   d. sulfur oxide

Hold the Fries (!)

. . . and the burger, and the bacon, and the eggs, and the chocolate sundae with whipped cream!

Heart disease used to be an old man's downfall, but the susceptible age line is steadily moving down. Now doctors are blaming our high cholesterol diet on the increased rate of heart disease.

We used to pity people in countries that survive on fish, beans, and vegetables. Now these foods are considered better dietary staples than the red meat and dairy products of the American diet.

High cholesterol is not only the cause of heart disease, but it is one that doctors are very sure of.

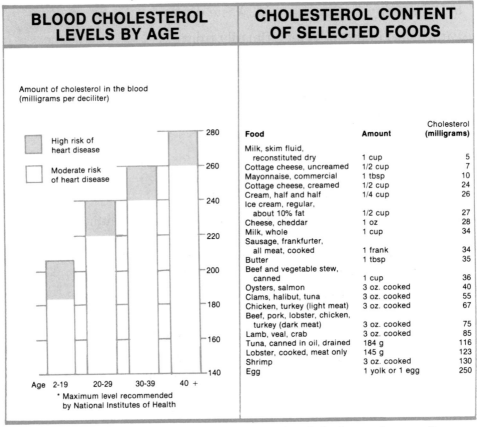

BLOOD CHOLESTEROL LEVELS BY AGE	CHOLESTEROL CONTENT OF SELECTED FOODS		

Amount of cholesterol in the blood (milligrams per deciliter)

High risk of heart disease

Moderate risk of heart disease

Food	Amount	Cholesterol (milligrams)
Milk, skim fluid, reconstituted dry	1 cup	5
Cottage cheese, uncreamed	1/2 cup	7
Mayonnaise, commercial	1 tbsp	10
Cottage cheese, creamed	1/2 cup	24
Cream, half and half	1/4 cup	26
Ice cream, regular, about 10% fat	1/2 cup	27
Cheese, cheddar	1 oz	28
Milk, whole	1 cup	34
Sausage, frankfurter, all meat, cooked	1 frank	34
Butter	1 tbsp	35
Beef and vegetable stew, canned	1 cup	36
Oysters, salmon	3 oz. cooked	40
Clams, halibut, tuna	3 oz. cooked	55
Chicken, turkey (light meat)	3 oz. cooked	67
Beef, pork, lobster, chicken, turkey (dark meat)	3 oz. cooked	75
Lamb, veal, crab	3 oz. cooked	85
Tuna, canned in oil, drained	184 g	116
Lobster, cooked, meat only	145 g	123
Shrimp	3 oz. cooked	130
Egg	1 yolk or 1 egg	250

Age   2-19   20-29   30-39   40 +

* Maximum level recommended by National Institutes of Health

The graph above shows the danger levels of cholesterol according to age groups. The table shows some surprising facts about the cholesterol contained in certain foods.

Use the graph and table on page 168 to answer these questions. Choose the correct answer.

1. How many milligrams of cholesterol in the blood would put someone under 20 years old in a high risk group for heart disease?
   a. 170
   b. 190
   c. 220
   d. 260

Check your answer. Find the bar graph for age 20. Check the key for the symbol on the graph. The answer is **b**.

2. What is the maximum level of cholesterol that would keep a 29-year-old person within the moderate risk category?
   a. 240 milligrams
   b. 200 milligrams
   c. over 220 milligrams
   d. less than 220 milligrams

3. How much cholesterol would you get from two fried eggs in two tablespoons of butter?
   a. 285 milligrams
   b. 570 milligrams
   c. 300 milligrams
   d. enough to kill you

4. Meat with the lowest milligrams of cholesterol is __.
   a. veal
   b. chicken
   c. lamb
   d. beef

5. Which food has almost double the cholesterol of the other?
   a. shrimp versus chicken
   b. lamb versus tuna
   c. eggs versus veal
   d. tuna fish versus sausage

6. How much more cholesterol does whole milk have than powdered skim milk?
   a. 19 milligrams
   b. 30 milligrams
   c. 29 milligrams
   d. 10 milligrams

7. From which foods would persons in the ages 2 to 19 group probably get too much cholesterol?
   a. seafoods
   b. whole milk and beef products
   c. raw vegetables
   d. all of them

8. The graph and table together are designed to warn people __.
   a. to eat less fat
   b. with heart disease
   c. on a fast food diet
   d. on special diet

Frequently, tests have questions that use visual materials such as maps, tables, and graphs. Use the visual materials as you follow the test tips on the next four pages. Put your answers on your answer sheet.

Test Tips: Study the map and table quickly. Read each question and use the right visual to answer it.

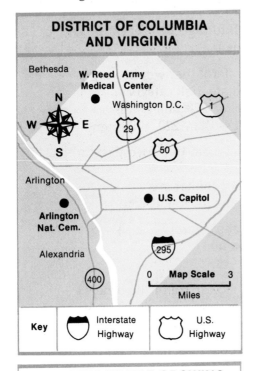

DISTRICT OF COLUMBIA AND VIRGINIA

LEADING WHEAT-GROWING STATES AND PROVINCES

	Bushels of wheat grown each year
Saskatchewan	521,750,000 bushels
Kansas	408,800,000 bushels
North Dakota	259,180,000 bushels
Alberta	221,500,000 bushels
Oklahoma	186,500,000 bushels
Montana	153,280,000 bushels

Key: = 50,000,000 bushels

Sources: U.S. Department of Agriculture; Statistics of Canada

Choose the best answer.

1. What interstate highway runs through the southeast section?
   a. 400   c. 1
   b. 295   d. 50

2. Arlington National Cemetery is about __ from the Capitol.
   a. 10 miles   c. 3 miles
   b. 30 miles   d. a mile

3. The W. Reed Army Medical Center is __ of the Capitol.
   a. north   c. east
   b. south   d. west

4. __ is the second major wheat producing area of North America.
   a. Kansas   c. Oklahoma
   b. Montana   d. Alberta

5. How many millions of bushels does Saskatchewan produce?
   a. 500   c. over 50
   b. over 500   d. under 500

6. About twice as much wheat is grown in __ as in Montana.
   a. Oklahoma
   b. North Dakota
   c. Kansas
   d. Alberta

Test Tips: Study the table carefully. Know what information it shows.

Test Tips: Answer the easier questions first. Then go back and do the harder ones.

UNION MEMBERSHIP IN THE UNITED STATES

Year	Total Workers (Nonagricultural)	Union Members	Per Cent In Unions
1930	29,424,000	3,401,000	12%
1935	27,053,000	3,584,000	13%
1940	32,376,000	8,717,000	27%
1945	40,394,000	14,322,000	36%
1950	45,222,000	14,267,000	32%
1955	50,675,000	16,802,000	33%
1960	54,234,000	17,049,000	31%
1965	60,815,000	17,299,000	28%
1970	70,920,000	19,381,000	27%
1975	76,945,000	19,564,000	25%
1978	85,763,000	20,238,000	24%

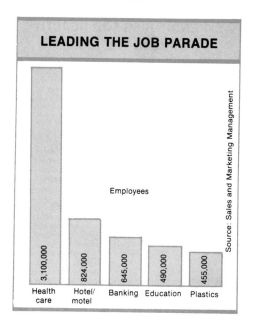

LEADING THE JOB PARADE

Employees

Source: Sales and Marketing Management

Health care	Hotel/motel	Banking	Education	Plastics
3,100,000	824,000	645,000	490,000	455,000

7. In 1975, what percent of the total work force were union members?
   a. 25%   c. 50%
   b. 30%   d. 75%

8. Between what years was the sharpest rise in union membership?
   a. 1935–1940   c. 1975–1978
   b. 1970–1975   d. 1955–1960

9. The highest percentage of union members in the work force was in __.
   a. 1978   c. 1970
   b. 1955   d. 1945

10. About how many people are employed in the field of lending and investing money?
    a. 11,000,000   c. 21,000,000
    b. 650,000,000   d. 600,000

11. The best job opportunities are in the __.
    a. computer research
    b. hotel management
    c. teaching
    d. medical arts

12. About __ more people are bankers than educators.
    a. 155,000   c. 8,000
    b. 7,000,000   d. 12,000

Test Tips: Be careful when using charts. Read the right set of numbers with the right category.

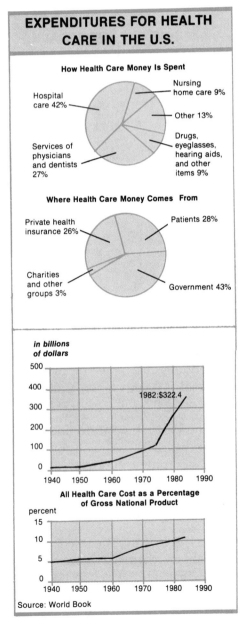

EXPENDITURES FOR HEALTH CARE IN THE U.S.

How Health Care Money Is Spent

Hospital care 42%
Nursing home care 9%
Other 13%
Drugs, eyeglasses, hearing aids, and other items 9%
Services of physicians and dentists 27%

Where Health Care Money Comes From

Private health insurance 26%
Patients 28%
Charities and other groups 3%
Government 43%

in billions of dollars

1982: $322.4

1940 1950 1960 1970 1980 1990

All Health Care Cost as a Percentage of Gross National Product

percent

1940 1950 1960 1970 1980 1990

Source: World Book

13. __ received the most health care dollars.
  a. Doctors
  b. Hospitals
  c. Insurance companies
  d. Nursing homes

14. About how much health care money comes from private health insurance?
  a. one-fourth   c. two-thirds
  b. one-half   d. one-third

15. Who pays the highest health care costs?
  a. government
  b. patients
  c. insurance companies
  d. charities

16. In 1960, health care was __ of the Gross National Product.
  a. 5%   c. 11%
  b. 12%   d. 7%

17. In 1982, the U.S. spent about __ billion dollars on health care.
  a. 100   c. 300
  b. 200   d. 322

18. Since 1970, the cost of health care has __.
  a. stabilized
  b. doubled
  c. increased slightly
  d. tripled

Directions: Use the graph and table to answer questions 19–21.

MOTOR VEHICLE TRAFFIC DEATHS IN THE U.S., 1980 - 1985

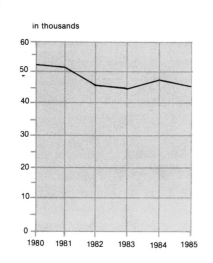

in thousands

Year	No. of Deaths
1980	52,600
1981	50,800
1982	46,000
1983	44,600
1984	46,200
1985	45,600

Source: National Safety Council

19. Which year had the highest number of fatalities?
   a. 1980   c. 1984
   b. 1982   d. 1985

20. About how many more people died in traffic accidents in 1981 than in 1982?
   a. 2,000   c. 10,000
   b. 5,000   d. 20,000

21. The graph indicates that traffic fatalities __.
   a. increased since 1980
   b. decreased since 1980
   c. decreased on alternate years since 1982
   d. stabilized at 50,000 per year

22. A __ map would show the volcanos in Hawaii.
   a. weather   c. product
   b. road   d. physical

23. Which visual aid would name the Americans' favorite musicians over the past 100 years?
   a. line graph   c. a chart
   b. a map   d. all of these

24. A __ would show the distance between cities on a road map.
   a. compass rose c. map key
   b. map scale   d. title

You will graduate from high school soon, and are scanning the "Help Wanted Ads" pages in the newspaper. An ad for a job in Vancouver, British Columbia, catches your attention.

The job description sounds like exciting work, an adventure with a future. It offers good pay and on-the-job training, but it is a long way from your home town. You should find out more about Vancouver before you start packing.

Where would you learn all the facts you need to know about living in British Columbia? There are many sources. Check them carefully before you make your decision. These are just a few of them.

A. Dictionary

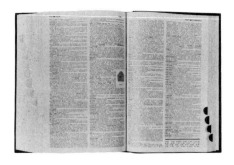

C. Almanacs

B. Encyclopedia

D. Books

E. Newspapers and Magazines

You don't have to read every page of every book, newspaper, and magazine to find the facts you need. But you have to know where to look. Ask the librarian to help you. Check yourself now to see how much you already know. Choose the best answer.

1. To learn the location of Vancouver, British Columbia, check the __.
   a. dictionary   c. almanac
   b. atlas   d. newspaper

2. Where would you best learn about the current population, climate, and government of Vancouver?
   a. dictionary   c. atlas
   b. almanac   d. encyclopedia

3. What source would list the principal industries in Vancouver?
   a. newspaper   c. magazine
   b. atlas   d. encyclopedia

On Your Own

Today, many young people find employment in a large company, learn some skills, and then become dissatisfied with working for others. They dream of opening their own business.

One way to do this is to purchase a *franchise,* or the rights to sell someone else's products. Businesses like McDonald's and Carvel are franchise operations. That is, the products they sell are owned by a corporation, but each store is managed by individual owners.

Franchises require varying amounts of start-up capital. If purchased from a reputable company, a franchise offers the opportunity for good income and advancement in the holding company.

However, operating a franchise demands a great deal of time and physical energy. In many cases, a franchiser has to manage several employees and a complex physical plant.

The word *franchise* is an interesting and exciting word in American business vocabulary. It appears on the dictionary page below.

---

fracture ● Franco

¹**frac·ture** \'frak-chər\ *n* **1 a :** the act or process of breaking or the state of being broken; *specif* : the breaking of hard tissue (as bone) **b :** the rupture of soft tissue **2 :** the result of fracturing : BREAK **3 :** the general appearance of a freshly broken surface of a mineral

frag·ment \'frag-mənt\ *n* [ME, fr. L *fragmentum,* fr. *frangere* to break — more at BREAK] : a part broken off, detached, or incomplete *syn* see PART

frame *n* **1 a :** something composed of parts fitted together and united **b :** the physical makeup of an animal and esp. a human body : PHYSIQUE, FIGURE **2 a :** the constructional system that gives shape or strength (as to a building); *also* : a frame dwelling **b :** such a skeleton not filled in or covered

¹**fran·chise** \'fran-,chīz\ *n* [ME, fr OF, fr *franchir* to free, fr *franc* free] **1 :** freedom or immunity from some burden or restriction vested in a person or group **2 a:** a special privilege granted to an individual or group; *esp* : the right to be and exercise the powers of a corporation **b :** a constitutional or statutory right or privilege; *esp* : the right to vote **c** (1) : the right or license granted to an individul or group to market a company's goods or services in a particular territory (2) : the territory involved in such a right

²**franchise** *vt* **fran·chised; fran·chis·ing 1** *archaic* : FREE **2 :** to grant a franchise to

fran·chi·see \,fran-,chī-'zē, -chə-\ *n* : one that is granted a franchise

fran·chis·er \'fran-,chī-zər\ *n* [in sense 1, fr. ¹*franchise;* in sense 2, fr. ²*franchise*] **1 :** FRANCHISEE **2 :** FRANCHISOR

fran·chi·sor \,fran-,chī-'zȯ(ə)r, -chə-\ *n* [²*franchise* + *-or*] : one that grants a franchise

Fran·cis·can \fran-'sis-kən\ *n* [ML *Franciscus* Francis] : a member of the Order of Friars Minor founded by St. Francis of Assisi in 1209 and dedicated esp. to preaching, missions, and charities

Franco- *comb form* [ML, fr. *Francus* Frenchman, fr. LL, Frank] : French and <*Franco*-German> : French <*Franco*phile>

Entries in a dictionary are listed in alphabetical order. In addition to the pronunciation of a word, the number of syllables, origin of the word, part of speech, and numbered meanings are also given.

Use the dictionary sample on page 176 to answer these questions. Choose the best answer.

1. The word *franchise* is listed twice. Its first meaning is listed as what part of speech?
   a. noun
   b. pronoun
   c. verb
   d. preposition

Check your answer. The letter *n* in italics appears immediately after the pronunciation. That letter stands for *noun*. The answer is **a**.

2. *Franchise* comes from a ME (Middle English) word which in turn came from the OF (Old French) word meaning ___.
   a. to flee
   b. to free
   c. to find
   d. to frame

3. Read all the definitions for *franchise*. Which definition would apply to someone seeking a business opportunity?
   a. 2-1
   b. 2-2
   c. 1-1
   d. 1-2c(1)

4. A ___ buys the rights to market somebody else's product.
   a. *franchise*
   b. *franchisee*
   c. *franchiser*
   d. *franchisor*

5. The word *Franciscan* is capitalized because it is ___.
   a. a person's name
   b. a proper noun
   c. the name of a group of people
   d. b and c

6. A hardware store might sell a window ___.
   a. *fragment*
   b. *fracture*
   c. *frame*
   d. *franchise*

7. Which definition of the word *frame* is used in this sentence? *The building inspector disapproved the proposed frame of the house.*
   a. **1a**
   b. **1b**
   c. **2a**
   d. **2b**

8. The word *Franco* is followed by a hyphen and the phrase *comb form.* This tells us that the word ___.
   a. can stand alone
   b. is of French origin
   c. is used only with another word
   d. is rarely used

Don't Shout!

But demand to be heard when you speak for your rights as a consumer. Every consumer has to know when a product is worth its price. When it is not, the consumer should take certain steps.

Suppose you sent for a record that was advertised on TV, and the record arrived damaged. What would you do? Or how would you deal with being overcharged on your electric bill?

To learn what your rights as a consumer are, and what action you can take to protect these rights, you might consult a textbook on civil justice. Check its table of contents and index, to see the kind of information you will find in the book.

A sample table of contents and part of an index from a civil law textbook is given below.

Use the table of contents and the part of the index on page 178 to answer these questions. Choose the best answer.

1. In which parts would you find information about signing a housing lease?
   a. Part 1 and Part 2
   b. Part 1 and Part 3
   c. Part 3 and Part 4
   d. Part 2 and Part 3

Check your answer. You sign a lease or a contract when you rent somebody else's property. The answer is **d**.

2. On which page would you find information about suing someone for libel (false statements)?
   a. 125
   b. 151
   c. 211
   d. 170

3. In which chapter would you find information about dealing with misleading advertising?
   a. Part 4, Chapter 9
   b. Part 1, Chapter 2
   c. Part 2, Chapter 5
   d. Part 1, Chapter 1

4. On which page would you find the term "class action" mentioned?
   a. 10
   b. 106
   c. 214
   d. 37

5. Which subject does the text cover most thoroughly?
   a. contracts
   b. criminal law
   c. breach of contract
   d. accidents

6. The type of law which covers consumer rights, advertising techniques and credit agreements is called ___.
   a. criminal law
   b. marriage law
   c. compulsory education law
   d. civil law

7. In which chapter would you find the definition of a contract?
   a. Chapter 3
   b. Chapter 1
   c. Chapter 8
   d. Chapter 5

8. Your employer refuses to pay you the amount specified in your contract. Find information about this on pages ___.
   a. 37–47
   b. 83–84
   c. 116–117
   d. 127–151

Looking Good!

Once upon a time some girls were born beautiful, and some were not so lucky. But today, any girl can be beautiful. Information about diet, health, exercise, and especially about cosmetology, is available to anyone.

More and more young people are finding cosmetology a satisfying career. Many vocational schools now offer certified instructions in cosmetology. And students find that they enjoy helping people to feel better about themselves.

In the library are many books on cosmetology. A popular one is *The Medically Based No-Nonsense Beauty Book*. Another is a book by Clare Miller. The library catalog cards for these books are given below.

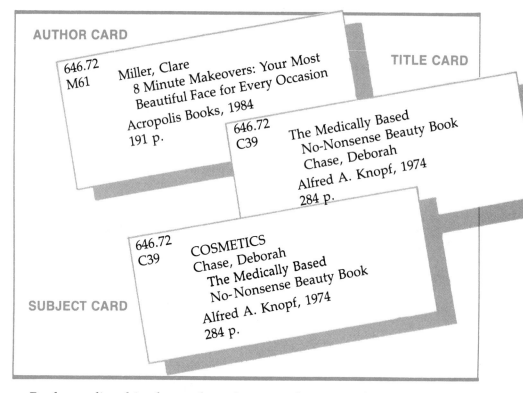

Books are listed in the card catalog according to author, subject and title. The number in the upper left corner of the card tells you that the book will be found on the shelf that holds books with the same 646 identification number.

Use the catalog cards on page 180 to answer these questions. Choose the best answer.

1. To find another book by Clare Miller, look under the letter ___.
   a. C   c. E
   b. M   d. F

Check your answer. Other books by Clare Miller would be listed under Miller, Clare. The answer is **b**.

2. Books on the famous cosmetologist, Estee Lauder, would be found in the card catalog drawer marked ___.
   a. M   c. C
   b. L   d. b and c

3. On what kind of card would you find information about hairstyles?
   a. author card   c. title card
   b. subject card   d. none of the cards

4. To learn if there is a book about people who are allergic to cosmetics, first check the card catalog drawer under ___.
   a. MEDICINE, ALLERGIES   c. COSMETICS, ALLERGIES
   b. Miller, Clare   d. ALLERGIES, SKIN

5. If you want a new look for the senior prom, check the ___ shelves.
   a. 200   c. 100
   b. 300   d. 600

6. Books on cosmetics would not be listed under which heading?
   a. clowns   c. theater
   b. face   d. music

7. To write to Clare Miller, you may address the letter to ___.
   a. Acropolis Books   c. your local library
   b. Alfred A. Knopf   d. Dalton's Book Store

8. Who is Alfred A. Knopf?
   a. a cosmetic manufacturer   c. an author
   b. a publisher   d. an editor

Keeping in Shape

One look in the mirror and you realize that you are out of shape. Not only are your muscles flabby, but your clothes don't fit properly either. It's time to shape up and move out into the world of physical fitness.

More and more Americans are exercising regularly. They are also spending a fortune to stay physically fit. In 1985, they spent two billion dollars for exercise shoes alone. Today, Americans are spending more—not only for exercise shoes and clothes, but also for expensive exercise gadgets.

To learn more about exercise, its health benefits as well as its hazards, you would read recent magazine articles. These are listed in the *Readers' Guide to Periodical Literature* in the library.

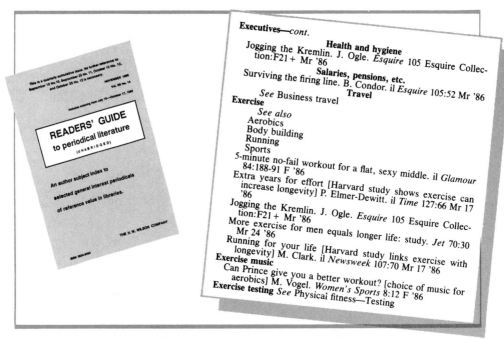

The *Readers' Guide to Periodical Literature* is a reference book that lists magazine articles. Articles are listed alphabetically by subject or author. Each subject entry in the *Readers' Guide* lists all the articles written on that subject in one year. The entry names the author, the magazine, and the pages on which the article is found. Most entries also give the volume number of the magazine before the page number.

182

Use the section of the *Readers' Guide* on page 182 to answer these questions. Choose the best answer.

1. Who wrote the article "Running For Your Life?"
   a. M. Vogel   c. M. Clark
   b. the editors of *Glamour*   d. J. Ogle

Check your answer. The author of the article is given after the title and sub-title. The answer is **c**.

2. When was the article "Extra Years for Extra Effort" published?
   a. March 17, 1986   c. May 24, 1986
   b. February, 1986   d. January, 1986

3. What other subject could be consulted for information about exercise?
   a. wrestling   c. weight lifting
   b. aerobics   d. testing

4. Which magazine gives information about exercising to music?
   a. *Glamour*   c. *Women's Sports*
   b. *Time*   d. *Newsweek*

5. Which entry does not give the author's name?
   a. "Jogging the Kremlin"
   b. "Can Prince Give You a Better Workout?"
   c. "Extra Years For Extra Effort"
   d. "More Exercise For Men Equals Longer Life"

6. Under what other heading besides Exercise would you find the article "Jogging the Kremlin?"
   a. Body Building   c. Executives
   b. Aerobics   d. Running

7. What letter should you turn to in order to find articles about athletic shoes?
   a. A   c. S
   b. R   d. J

8. On what page of *Glamour* would you find an article on flattening your tummy?
   a. 84   c. 86
   b. 91   d. 188

Passing on the Olympic Torch

The first Olympic games were held almost 3,400 years ago in Greece. The ancient Greeks are said to have held them as part of funeral ceremonies because they believed that physical activity was a wholesome outlet for the extreme emotion of grief.

However, the games continued as competitive sports for centuries. When countries were at war, fighting was stopped while the games were in progress. It was unthinkable to attack anyone who was on his way to the Olympics.

When Rome conquered Greece in 394 A.D., the games were abandoned and were not resumed until 1896. A French educator, Baron de Coubertin, later restored the Olympics on an international scale in order to encourage world peace.

An encyclopedia can give you more interesting facts about the Olympics—its history, the players and the countries which won the most medals, and the records made and broken.

INDEX

Olivier, Laurence [British actor] **O:564**
  with portrait
  Motion Picture (Best Actor) **M:718**
  Shakespeare, William (Modern Performances) **S:295** with picture
Olmedo, Alex [American tennis player]
  Tennis (Table) **T:132**
Olympia [region, Greece] **O:565**
  Olympic Games **O:566**; (The Ancient Games) **O:570**
Olympic Games O:566 with pictures
  Circus **Ci:436**
  Decathlon **D:58**
  Discus Throw **D:180**
  Greece, Ancient (Religion) **G:362**
  Hockey (Amateur Development) **H:250**

Homing Pigeon (History) **H:274**
Horse Racing (Early Horse Racing) **H:332**
Judo (History) **J:149**
Marathon **M:150**
Olympia **O:565**
Peace (Ancient Greece and Rome) **P:182**
Russia (Russia Today) **R:527**
Track and Field **T:277**
Omar Khayyam [Persian poet] **O:574**
  Algebra (History) **A:343**
  Rubaiyat **R:459**
Omar Khayyam [horse]
  Kentucky Derby (table) **K:232**

Study the sample part of an encyclopedia index given above. Each entry shows a topic with the letter of the encyclopedia volume followed by the page number.

Use the information on page 184 to answer these questions. Choose the best answer.

1. In which lettered volume and on which page would you find facts about the Olympic games?
   a. O:277   c. O:140
   b. O:566   d. O:250

Check your answer. Articles on the Olympics are listed in the index under O on page 566. The answer is **b.**

2. How many articles on the Olympic games does the index list?
   a. 10   c. 4
   b. 14   d. 8

3. In which other volume besides O and on what page would you find information about Judo?
   a. D:180   c. T:277
   b. J:565   d. J:149

4. Where would you look for information on Russia's role in the Olympics?
   a. Volumes O and R   c. Volumes D and R
   b. Volumes R and G   d. Volumes G and O

5. Which of the following topics does not give information related to the Olympic games?
   a. Discus Throw   c. Kentucky Derby
   b. Greece, Ancient   d. Marathon

6. Laurence Olivier was a great British stage and film actor. In which volumes would you find details about his performances?
   a. Volumes M, O, S   c. Volumes L, O, S
   b. Volumes A, L, O   d. Volumes B, O, S

7. Information about Alex Olmedo, the American tennis player, can be found in __.
   a. Volume O, page 119   c. Volume T, page 98
   b. Volume A, page 232   d. Volume T, page 132

8. Omar Khayyam is the name of a Persian poet. Where would you find information about a race horse named after him?
   a. Volume R, page 459   c. Volume O, page 574
   b. Volume K, page 232   d. Volume H, page 19

LESSON 6

Passage to India

The movie, *Passage to India*, gave the world a glimpse of the often turbulent history of India. Today, India remains an exotic, vast and troubled part of South Asia. One-third the size of the United States, India has thrice the U.S. population. By the year 2000, India is projected to have one billion people. Sikh extremists are violently seeking their own homeland—*Khalistan* or *Land of the Pure*—in the state of Punjab. Prime Minister Indira Gandhi was assassinated in 1984 by two of her Sikh bodyguards. Mahatma (*Great Soul*) Gandhi, who led a "civil disobedience" movement to end British rule, was assassinated in 1948. But India is also a land of mystics, poets and peace lovers. Indira's son, Rajiv, a pilot, is now steering the country through the turbulence of the modern age.

The map below shows where India is located.

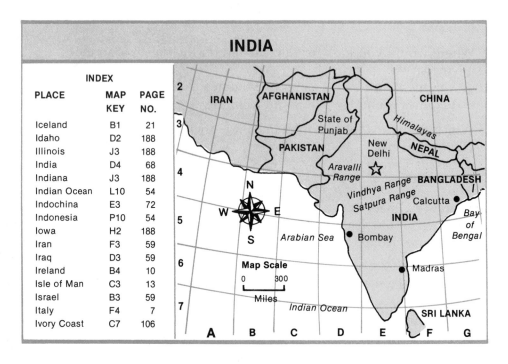

An atlas is a reference book that contains maps of many places. It also gives geographical facts. An index at the back of an atlas lists all the places on all the maps and tells where each can be found.

186

Use the map and index on page 186 to answer the following questions. Choose the best answer.

1. What is the letter/number key used to find India on the map?
   a. B2
   b. C2
   c. D4
   d. 112

Check your answer. Look up "India" in the index. The index gives the letter/number coordinates of India. Look at the map of India to check the coordinates. The answer is **c.**

2. On what page of the atlas can this map of India be found?
   a. 54
   b. 68
   c. 72
   d. D4

3. What mountain range separates India from China?
   a. Aravalli Range
   b. Satpura Range
   c. Himalayas
   d. Vindhya Range

4. What country shares its border with India on the western side?
   a. Afghanistan
   b. Bangladesh
   c. China
   d. Pakistan

5. On what page would you find a map of the Isle of Man?
   a. C3
   b. 10
   c. 12
   d. 13

6. What page number and letter/number key are given for Iowa?
   a. page 188, D2
   b. page 59, D3
   c. page 188, H2
   d. page 21, 81

7. What city in India is nearest to Bangladesh?
   a. New Delhi
   b. Calcutta
   c. Madras
   d. Bombay

8. What country lies at the southern tip of India?
   a. Afghanistan
   b. Sri Lanka
   c. Bangladesh
   d. Nepal

Tax Information

Most Americans have to file an income tax by April 15th of each year. Some people hire accountants or other professionals to fill out the returns. Others must struggle with the forms themselves and hope they have coordinated the right numbers with the right lines.

But did you know that the almanac can help you in filing your income tax return? A guide to preparing your income tax is found in the almanac.

CONSUMER SURVIVAL KIT

Your Federal Income Tax: Facts on Filing
Who Must File

A taxpayer with gross income of less than $3,430 (or less than $4,470 if 65 or older) should file a return to claim the refund of any taxes withheld, even if he or she is listed as a dependent by another taxpayer.

Forms to Use

A taxpayer may, at his or her election, use form 1040, form 1040A or form 1040EZ. However, those taxpayers who choose to itemize deductions must use the longer form 1040. The 1040EZ can be used only by qualifying single taxpayers.

New Tax Changes for 1984 and After

• **Distilled Spirits.** The excise tax on distilled spirits is $10.50 per proof gallon. Beginning rate of tax October 1, 1985, has been increased to $12.50 per proof gallon.

Dates for Filing Returns

For individuals using the calendar year, Apr. 15 is the final date (unless it falls on a Saturday, Sunday, or a legal holiday) for filing income tax returns and paying any tax due, and for paying the first quarterly installment of the estimated tax. Other installments of estimated tax are to be paid by June 15, Sept. 15, and Jan. 15.

Joint Return

A husband and wife may file a joint return, even if one has no income.

Exemptions

Personal exemption is $1,040. Every individual has an exemption of $1,040, to be deducted from gross income. A husband and a wife are each entitled to a $1,040 exemption. A taxpayer or spouse who is 65 or over on the last day of the year gets another exemption of $1,040. A husband or wife who is blind on the last day of the year gets another exemption of $1,040.

An almanac is a reference book that has many facts on both history and current events. The almanac is revised each year and contains information under various headings. These headings are listed in the index. The facts in an almanac, however, are not as extensive as the information which you would find in an encyclopedia or in a book devoted to a particular topic.

Use the parts of the almanac on page 188 to answer these questions. Choose the best answer.

1. If a taxpayer chooses to itemize deductions, he must use form ___.
  a. 1040A
  b. 1040Z
  c. 1040
  d. 1050

Check your answer. Find the heading for Tax Forms. Find the sentence about itemized deductions. The answer is **c**.

2. Who may file a joint return (two people filing the same form)?
  a. an engaged couple
  b. a brother and sister
  c. a husband and wife
  d. no one

3. The Tax Reform Act of 1984 ___.
  a. reduced local telephone rates
  b. raised the tax on alcoholic beverages
  c. doubled alimony rates
  d. increased salary deductions

4. April 15th is the final date for filing a tax return unless ___.
  a. you are filing a joint account
  b. you are an astronaut in space
  c. it falls on a legal holiday
  d. you earn over $100,000

5. How much money must you earn in a year before you are required to file a return and pay income tax?
  a. not exceeding $5,500
  b. a minimum of $3,500
  c. $3,430 or less
  d. $3,430 or more

6. How much money must your grandfather over the age of 65 earn in a year before he must file a return and pay income tax?
  a. $4,470
  b. $4,000
  c. $2,100
  d. $1,500

7. The amount of personal exemption is ___.
  a. $2,200
  b. $2,280
  c. $1,040
  d. $1,500

8. You are entitled to a refund if you earn ___.
  a. less than $3,430
  b. more than $4,000
  c. less than your spouse
  d. more than your spouse

Farm Crisis

During the Depression, the Department of Agriculture set up programs to control farm production and keep farm prices up. Since then, however, the farmer's troubles have multiplied. Surpluses have piled up. Government subsidies (payment to farmers) have made farm goods too costly to compete in the world market.

On the left is a newspaper report on this topic. On the right is a magazine article which concentrates on more than just the facts surrounding the farm crisis.

NEWSPAPER ARTICLE	MAGAZINE ARTICLE
"It's worse than it has been before" Another local tractor company closed this weekend and increased the financial pressures on the small rural community. "There won't be a town here anymore if this keeps up," said one resident. With many of its 5,000 residents working only on seasonal jobs, and others unemployed altogether, the town is struggling for survival. "It's worse than it has been before," said another resident. "It's bad for everybody." An important study commission has warned that the simultaneous decline of manufacturing and agriculture spells a terrible disaster for all the South, for the sparkling cities like Atlanta and Louisville as well as for the dirt-poor towns that are wrestling with poverty and unemployment. 	***STRESS TAKES ITS TOLL*** Many farmers, affected by the low prices paid for their products and the high debts they have incurred, are watching a cherished way of life slip away from them. A Congressional study predicts that more than a million family farms may vanish. These will be replaced by "superfarms," farms large enough to incorporate new technology like genetic engineering. Such predictions tend to make farmers very angry. And very frightened. The rates of depression, suicide, alcoholism and broken families have risen in rural America as well as the sale of guns. Children of farmers are also feeling the pain. Some of them will refuse a new pair of shoes, thinking this is something they can do to save the farm. Meanwhile, farm families live in a state of uneasiness. Not knowing whose farm will be lost next, everyone expects the worse and no one knows how to make things better.

A newspaper article has very current information. It gives the basic facts by answering the questions who, what, where, when, and why. A magazine article can give more details and more background information. However, it is not as up-to-date as a newspaper article.

Use the articles on page 190 to answer these questions. Choose the best answer.

1. The newspaper article does not tell you about ___.
   a. western farmers   c. farm children
   b. farm subsidies   d. all of these

Check your answer. All of these topics are mentioned in the magazine article only. The answer is **d.**

2. Which article has emotional appeal?
   a. the newspaper article   c. both a and b
   b. the magazine article   d. neither a nor b

3. Where could you find some background history on the U.S. farming industry?
   a. encyclopedia   c. almanac
   b. science magazine   d. atlas

4. Where would you find what has been written on farm subsidies since 1984?
   a. newspaper   c. *Readers' Guide*
   b. encyclopedia   d. almanac

5. Where would you find statistics on recent farm production?
   a. science magazine   c. encyclopedia
   b. almanac   d. all of these

6. Where would you find a weather map of farm areas in the U.S.?
   a. almanac   c. encyclopedia
   b. newspaper   d. atlas

7. The newspaper article ___.
   a. discusses the plight of rural farms
   b. ignores the problem of unemployment
   c. predicts the development of "super farms"
   d. all of these

8. The magazine article ___.
   a. quotes a Congressional study
   b. ignores the problem of farm children
   c. refers to farm equipment
   d. deals only with rural farms

Any Which Way You Can

The U.S. Department of Agriculture knows from years of research and experimentation that certain imported meats can carry such serious viral diseases as hoof-and-mouth or African swine fever. In order to prevent these diseases from coming into the country, the government doesn't turn to Rambo. It uses Jackpot, a 24-pound beagle.

Jackpot begins his day sniffing for food and plants at New York's JFK Airport by having his teeth brushed. He then swallows a vitamin pill and is dressed in his green coat that is stamped "Protecting U.S. Agriculture." Officially, Jackpot is Agent 0-1-D in the Beagle Brigade, a canine force trained by the Department of Agriculture to sniff out foods which are brought into the U.S. illegally by travelers.

For most of us information is gathered, not by sniffing, but by using reference materials. Once you decide what facts you need, you can then determine which reference materials will give you those facts.

Choose the best answer.

1. Which source would be the best place to find current information on using dogs in law enforcement?
   a. atlas
   c. magazine
   b. encyclopedia
   d. dictionary

Check your answer. A magazine has articles on topics of current interest. The answer is **c.**

2. Which source would give you the names of your congressmen?
   a. *Readers' Guide*
   c. almanac
   b. newspaper
   d. card catalog

3. Where would you look first to find information about restoring the Statue of Liberty?
   a. encyclopedia
   c. *Readers' Guide*
   b. dictionary
   d. atlas

4. What source would most likely list the number of people employed in the U.S. last year?
   a. almanac
   c. *Readers' Guide*
   b. encyclopedia
   d. newspaper

5. If you wanted to find a book on car repair, where would you look?
   a. *Readers' Guide*
   c. card catalog
   b. encyclopedia
   d. almanac index

6. Which would be the most likely place to find a definition of the word *canine*?
   a. encyclopedia
   c. dictionary
   b. almanac
   d. card catalog

7. Where would you look to find the distance between Australia and Africa?
   a. encyclopedia
   c. *Readers' Guide*
   b. almanac
   d. atlas

8. Which of these sources would have information about current career opportunities?
   a. social studies textbook
   c. encyclopedia
   b. business magazine
   d. almanac

Practice your reference skills as you follow the test tips on the next three pages. Put your answers on your answer sheet.

Test Tips: Read each answer choice carefully. Then, narrow your choices. Eliminate wrong answers until you are left with only the correct answer.

Choose the word that would come first in alphabetical order.

1. a. Prentiss, Alan
   b. Pollard, James
   c. Pritchard, Ellen
   d. Pratt, Elizabeth

2. a. zodiac
   b. zirconium
   c. zipcode
   d. zombie

3. a. Himalaya
   b. Hindustan
   c. Hirosaki
   d. Hialeah

4. a. staunch
   b. steadfast
   c. status
   d. stationery

Test Tips: Study the reference material shown before you read the questions.

Use the dictionary entry below to answer questions 5-7.

ma·ture (mə toor', -tyoor', -choor'), *adj., v.* **-tured, -turing.** —*adj.* **1.** complete in natural growth or development, as plant and animal forms. **2.** ripe, as fruit, or fully aged, as cheese, wine, etc. **3.** fully developed in body or mind, as a person. **4.** pertaining to or characteristic of full development. **5.** completed, perfected, or elaborated in full by the mind: *mature plans.* **6.** *Phys. Geog.* (of topographical features) exhibiting the stage of maximum stream development, as in the process of erosion of a land surface. —*v.t.* **7.** to make mature; ripen. **8.** to bring to full development. **9.** to complete or perfect. —*v.i.* **10.** to become mature; ripen. **11.** to come to full development. **12.** *Finance,* to become due, as a note. [late ME < L *mātur(us)* ripe, timely, early; akin to MANES] —**ma·ture'ly,** *adv.* —**ma·ture'ness,** *n.* —**Syn. 1, 3.** aged, grown, adult. **2.** See **ripe.**

5. The word *mature* is what part of speech?
   a. noun   c. verb
   b. adjective   d. b an c

6. What was the meaning of *mature* in Middle English?
   a. morning   c. afternoon
   b. ripe   d. adult

7. Which definition of *matured* is used in this sentence? *Her harsh judgment of people changed as she matured.*
   a. 1   c. 4
   b. 2   d. 3

Test Tips: Sometimes, it helps to use the reference material shown to answer the question *before* you look at the answer choices. Then, you can check yourself by finding your answer among the choices.

Here is the table of contents from a textbook called *Two Centuries of Progress*. Use it to answer questions 8-9.

CONTENTS	Page

8. Which chapter would have information on Abraham Lincoln?
a. 5   c. 2
b. 3   d. 4

9. Which pages would you read to learn about the founding of the United Nations?
a. 96-220   c. 289-320
b. 364-388   d. 360-364

Here is part of the index from the same book. Use it to answer questions 10-13.

INDEX

Airplanes and aircraft industry: 447,491. See also Aerospace research and industry.
Automation: 646-647, ill. 575

Chinese in America: 689-690
Culture: influences on American, 283-284, of the U.S., 269-273

Education: and television, 667
Industry: automation, 646-647

Political Parties: beginnings of, 146-148; definition of, 138

Women: education for, 247, 407; right to vote, 507-515

10. On what page can you learn what a Democrat is?
a. 283   c. 138
b. 689   d. 491

11. Which listing gives a further reference?
a. Political Parties   c. Culture
b. Women   d. Airplanes

12. What page talks about the effects of media on education?
a. 247   c. 283
b. 667   d. 575

13. Robots would be discussed on pages ___.
a. 646-647   c. 283-284
b. 689-690   d. 146-148

Test Tips: Most study skills tests include questions about the purpose of each type of reference material. Read each question carefully. Be sure to answer what is being asked—not what you think should be asked.

14. Which would be the best source for a diagram of the solar system?
    a. dictionary   c. encyclopedia
    b. almanac   d. newspaper

15. Which source would give you the winners of the 1985 Summer Olympic games?
    a. encyclopedia
    b. almanac
    c. newspaper
    d. card catalog

16. To find a short story by O.Henry, check the __.
    a. almanac
    b. encyclopedia
    c. card catalog
    d. magazine

17. To research a topic on Vietnam, use the __.
    a. almanac index
    b. *Readers' Guide*
    c. encyclopedia
    d. all of these

18. In *Bride Magazine,* where would you find which pages have facts about honeymoons?
    a. table of contents
    b. card catalog
    c. *Readers' Guide*
    d. almanac

19. Where would you find the 1986 boundaries of Lebanon and Israel?
    a. almanac   c. encyclopedia
    b. atlas   d. dictionary

20. In *The History of Music,* where would you look first to find all the information on rock music in England?
    a. table of contents   c. index
    b. dictionary   d. glossary

21. Which reference would list the names of magazine articles written on employment opportunities?
    a. card catalog
    b. *Readers' Guide*
    c. atlas
    d. science magazine

22. Where would you find the names of the heads of the major American political parties?
    a. encyclopedia   c. dictionary
    b. atlas   d. almanac

23. Where would you find yesterday's World Series scores?
    a. *Sports Illustrated*
    b. card catalog
    c. newspaper
    d. *Readers' Guide*

UNIT IV
TESTS

Test 1

Test 2

READING COMPREHENSION

Directions: This test will show how well you understand what you read. Read each passage. Then do the items that follow it. Choose the best answer for each item. On your answer sheet, fill in the space that goes with the answer you choose.

When you open the menu in any ethnic restaurant, what common dish will you find? *Frijoles Refritos* (refried beans) from Mexico, *Cocido* (beef and chick peas) from Spain, *Faviola Toscan* (bean and pasta soup) from Italy, *Hummus* (seasoned crushed chick peas) from the Middle East, and *Curried Lentils* from India are all made from a common source of high energy nutrients: the *legume*.

Legumes are plants that belong to the pea family. The name means pea pod. There are between 14,000 and 17,000 species of legumes, including trees, shrubs, and herbs. The Native Americans have long recognized the value of these plants which not only grow in soil that is too poor to support corn, but also produces food that could be stored for the winter.

Dr. Robert Haas, a nutritionist who has worked with many famous athletes like Martina Navratilova, has recommended that all women eat between three and seven cups of beans, peas, or lentils a week. He says these legumes contain a high percentage of iron, protein, mineral, and fiber. Any food with such nutritional value will definitely become popular in health-conscious America.

---

1. The phrase *common source of nutrients* suggests that legumes are __.
   a. new to Americans
   b. found almost everywhere
   c. part of the regular diet
   d. a popular nutritious food

2. This article is mainly about the __ of legumes.
   a. varieties
   b. nutritional value
   c. history
   d. fiber content

3. The first paragraph suggests that legumes have been the source of nutrition among __.
   a. non-Americans   c. gourmets
   b. farmers   d. vegetarians

4. Which of the legume's values was most important to the Native Americans?
   a. Its high protein content.
   b. It is easy to cook.
   c. It is easily stored for the winter.
   d. Its high iron content.

The longest explored cave in the world, Mammoth Cave, consists of 200 miles of underground passageways south of Louisville, Kentucky. It is located in a mountain range composed mostly of limestone. Over hundreds of years, the water above ground seeped into the earth. As it trickled through the hollows of the earth, it eroded the rock and limestone and formed the Mammoth Cave.

The largest chamber inside the cave, the Chief Temple, measures 125 feet high by 500 feet long and 300 feet wide. It was used as a meeting place by Native Americans who lived nearby. Their torches and weapons have been found in the room.

Each chamber has interesting formations. In Star Chamber, crystals of white gypsum "sparkle" against a "sky" of black manganese. In Charlotte's Grotto, insects hum and buzz behind crystal arches.

Frozen Niagara is another amazing sight. The limestone on one of the walls looks like a gigantic waterfall. In fact, much of this underground world resembles the world above ground. Formations in the cave look like waterfalls, flowers, and trees. Even Echo River that winds through the cave holds fish that seem familiar. These are "blindfish." They have no eyes; feelers on their bodies give them a sense of touch. Many tourists are surprised to find many similarities between life in these underground passages and that above ground.

---

5. Frozen Niagara apparently got its name because of its resemblance to __.
   a. a woman
   b. an icy river
   c. Niagara Falls
   d. a blind fish

6. The largest chamber inside the Mammoth Cave is the __.
   a. Chief Temple
   b. Star Chamber
   c. Charlotte's Grotto
   d. Frozen Niagara

7. The information given is mostly about the __.
   a. cave's history
   b. cave's chambers
   c. life above ground
   d. formation of caves

8. The most appropriate title for the passage is __.
   a. "The Longest Cave"
   b. "Frozen Niagara"
   c. "Mammoth Cave"
   d. "Cave Chambers"

An editorial: Year-round schools make good sense. They are the answer to rising costs in education. The present school calendar was designed primarily to serve the agricultural economy of the 19th century. That economy has changed.

A popular schedule seems to be nine weeks of school followed by three weeks of vacation. This is repeated three more times which leaves about four weeks to be used as vacation or for further schooling. Schedules are staggered so that at any one time, one-fourth of the student body is on vacation. This plan allows communities to educate more students without raising taxes to build more schools. All those in favor of lower taxes should welcome this proposal.

A letter of reply: Year-round schools do not meet all the needs of the family, the students, or the community. Children from the same family may have different schedules, thus creating extra problems for "latchkey" children whose parents work during the day. It also creates problems in planning family vacations, interrupts extracurricular activities, and makes participation in team sports almost impossible.

With so many children out of school at different times, truancy will be a problem. How is anyone to know who should be on the street and who should be in school? Any savings in taxes will be used to pay the police instead of the teachers. So much for cheaper education!

---

9. Which of these is not an issue against year-round schools?
   a. overcrowding
   b. vacation problems
   c. lower taxes
   d. truancy

10. The editorial writer expects year-round schools to meet the needs of __.
    a. educators
    b. today's communities
    c. 19th century farmers
    d. the government

11. Which of these is least important to the letter writer?
    a. truancy
    b. athletic programs
    c. lower taxes
    d. "latchkey" children

12. The letter writer is apparently concerned with __.
    a. political issues
    b. economic issues
    c. human issues
    d. regional issues

Read the passage and the answer choices that follow it. Choose the best answer to complete each blank.

I have always loved dolphins. They are the most fascinating underwater creatures I know. _13_ they are swift and strong enough to kill a shark if necessary, they are very friendly to humans and are willing to interact with them. They even seem to talk among themselves in their language of clicks and whistles. People who train dolphins say they are generally tame and _14_ in captivity. However, there is one serious problem: dolphins are easily bored, probably because they are so _15_.

One family that operates a training school for dolphins has found one solution to this problem. For a fee of twenty-five dollars a half hour, they _16_ swimmers to put on flippers and slip into the water to play with their eight dolphins. They make money, the dolphins are _17_, and the people are fascinated.

Even though they can be frightening because of their huge size, when a dolphin comes up with its rubbery nose to give a kiss or nuzzle an arm, the swimmer realizes how friendly they really are. They roll over to be patted and fly through the air to show off. The biggest thrill is being allowed to grab a fin and to be towed at incredible speed. In only a few minutes, I was convinced that dolphins have a real, if mysterious, _18_ of human beings.

---

13. a. Since   c. Whenever
     b. Although   d. Because

14. a. wild   c. playful
     b. rough   d. hostile

15. a. fat   c. mobile
     b. big   d. intelligent

16. a. charge   c. allow
     b. encourage   d. hire

17. a. trained   c. annoyed
     b. bathed   d. entertained

18. a. treatment   c. dislike
     b. imitation   d. understanding

VOCABULARY

Directions: This test will show if you can recognize words that have the same meaning, words that have opposite meanings, and words that have several meanings. Mark your answers on your answer sheet.

For items 1-10, choose the word or phrase that means the same, or almost the same, as the word in dark type.

1. **initiate** a program
   a. stop
   b. start
   c. continue
   d. complete

2. an **unassuming** person
   a. innocent
   b. humble
   c. proud
   d. interesting

3. **profoundly** moved
   a. deeply
   b. slightly
   c. never
   d. almost

4. **cultivate** an interest
   a. begin
   b. develop
   c. encourage
   d. destroy

5. a terrible **menace**
   a. position
   b. person
   c. threat
   d. ending

6. a strange **phenomenon**
   a. attitude
   b. happening
   c. person
   d. habit

7. **surmise** the truth
   a. know
   b. think
   c. guess
   d. speak

8. **heed** a warning
   a. disregard
   b. obey
   c. understand
   d. give

9. a **pragmatic** reason
   a. wise
   b. idealistic
   c. practical
   d. correct

10. **revolutionize** an industry
    a. finance
    b. improve
    c. change
    d. destroy

For items 11-20, choose the word or phrase that means the opposite of the word in dark type.

11. **tampered** with it
    a. meddled
    b. finished
    c. left it alone
    d. played

12. a **significant** detail
    a. strange
    b. unimportant
    c. critical
    d. small

13. **debunking** the opposition
    a. praising
    b. ridiculing
    c. following
    d. destroying

14. a **celestial** object
    a. earthly
    b. heavenly
    c. starry
    d. beautiful

15. a **feigned** illness
    a. terrible
    b. pretended
    c. real
    d. fatal

16. a **unique** statue
    a. beautiful
    b. rare
    c. common
    d. clever

17. a **gullible** child
    a. doubting
    b. believing
    c. troubled
    d. innocent

18. a **competent** worker
    a. skillful
    b. reliable
    c. careful
    d. incapable

19. an **alleged** criminal
    a. accused
    b. convicted
    c. named
    d. charged

20. the **enchanting** castle
    a. uninteresting
    b. fascinating
    c. story-book
    d. ancient

For items 21-28, choose the sentence in which the word in dark type means the same as the definition given.

21. tool
  a. The politician was able to **implement** her plan for improving roads.
  b. Use a sharp **implement** to open this box.
  c. It isn't always easy to **implement** new ideas.

22. a firm hold
  a. It's easy to lose a package or **grip** on an airplane.
  b. She has obviously lost her **grip** on the situation.
  c. To open, **grip** the handle and pull hard.

23. a cafeteria in an army post
  a. Bob Hope entertained the soldiers at the **canteen.**
  b. The hiker carried only a small **canteen** of water.
  c. Pack the silverware neatly in the **canteen.**

24. increase in value
  a. The **appreciation** of these paintings increased when the artist died.
  b. A note of **appreciation** is always in good taste.
  c. His **appreciation** of nature made him a good poet.

25. a kind act
  a. Each guest received a **favor** at the bridal shower.
  b. You seem to **favor** your mother more than your father.
  c. Do me a **favor** and find some place else to play.

26. a building for animals
  a. The economy remained **stable** inspite of the war.
  b. A pig lives in a sty, not in a **stable**.
  c. He has a pleasant and **stable** personality.

27. to move clumsily
  a. **Lumbering** is difficult work after a forest fire.
  b. A gorilla's **lumbering** can be funny—from a distance!
  c. The **lumbering** and rattling of the movers annoyed me.

28. start something
  a. The cruise ship was too large to reach without a **launch.**
  b. You need more money to **launch** an enterprise.
  c. One **launch** followed another in the Liberty Weekend celebration.

Directions: This test will show how well you can find and use information from maps, tables, graphs, and reference materials. Read each question. Four answer choices are given, but only one is right. Fill in the space for the best answer on your answer sheet.

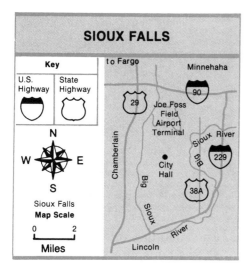

SIOUX FALLS

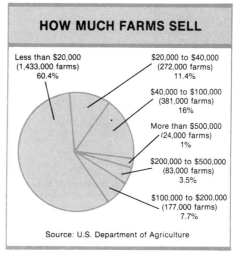

HOW MUCH FARMS SELL

Source: U.S. Department of Agriculture

1. U.S. Highway ___ runs east–west across the northern part of Sioux Falls.
   a. 90   c. 38A
   b. 229   d. 29

2. You travel ___ to go from Lincoln to Minnehaha.
   a. northeast   c. east
   b. southwest   d. northwest

3. About how far is it from the airport terminal to City Hall?
   a. 10 miles   c. 6 miles
   b. 2 miles   d. 18 miles

4. What city is west of the Big Sioux River where it crosses U.S. Highway 90?
   a. Lincoln   c. Minnehaha
   b. Fargo   d. Chamberlain

5. 60% of the total number of farms sell their output for ___.
   a. over $20,000   c. $40,000
   b. under $20,000   d. $100,000

6. 1% of the farms sell output valued at ___.
   a. over $500,000
   b. under $40,000
   c. 11.4% of produce
   d. under $400,000

7. 39.6% of the farms produce ___.
   a. over $100,000
   b. under $20,000
   c. $500,000
   d. $20,000 or more

8. Perhaps most farms do not ___.
   a. sell well   c. need help
   b. sell a lot   d. earn enough

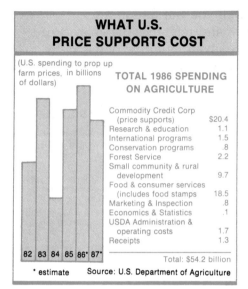

WHAT U.S. PRICE SUPPORTS COST

(U.S. spending to prop up farm prices, in billions of dollars)

82 83 84 85 86* 87*

* estimate   Source: U.S. Department of Agriculture

TOTAL 1986 SPENDING ON AGRICULTURE

Commodity Credit Corp (price supports)	$20.4
Research & education	1.1
International programs	1.5
Conservation programs	.8
Forest Service	2.2
Small community & rural development	9.7
Food & consumer services (includes food stamps	18.5
Marketing & Inspection	.8
Economics & Statistics	.1
USDA Administration & operating costs	1.7
Receipts	1.3
Total:	54.2 billion

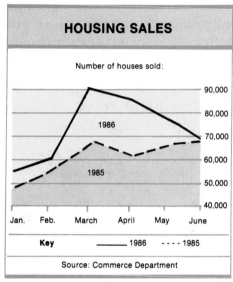

HOUSING SALES

Number of houses sold:

90,000
80,000
70,000
60,000
50,000
40,000

1986

1985

Jan. Feb. March April May June

Key ——— 1986   - - - - 1985

Source: Commerce Department

9. Government spending to support farm prices was the least in ___.
   a. 1987   c. 1986
   b. 1982   d. 1984

10. Support for farm prices cost the most in ___.
    a. 1986   c. 1985
    b. 1987   d. 1983

11. The total estimated 1986 budget for agriculture was ___.
    a. $10 million   c. $20 billion
    b. $54 million·   d. $54 billion

12. The second lowest budgeted item was for ___.
    a. price supports
    b. forest services
    c. marketing and inspection
    d. economics and statistics

13. The solid line on the graph shows housing sales for ___.
    a. March 1985   c. April, 1985
    b. 1985 and   d. part of
       1986   1986

14. About how many more homes were sold in February, 1986 than in February, 1985?
    a. 5,000   c. 1,000
    b. 50,000   d. 30,000

15. Housing sales were highest in ___.
    a. March, 1985   c. April, 1986
    b. March, 1986   d. June, 1985

16. The line graph shows that housing sales ___ or fluctuate up or down.
    a. rarely swing   c. never swing
    b. swing   d. seasonally
                         swing

CUSTOMS AND CULTURES

17. What chapter would discuss the problems of stepchildren?
    a. 1   c. 7
    b. 9   d. 13

18. In which part would you read about laws?
    a. C   c. D
    b. A   d. B

19. Entertainers have a great influence on fashion. This phenomenon might be discussed in Chapter __.
    a. 10   c. 3
    b. 13   d. 7

20. Which pages are about a society's literature?
    a. 58-64   c. 3-5
    b. 19-21   d. 65-68

Directions: Answer questions 21-25 about reference materials.

21. Which would you consult about the best route from San Antonio to Dallas?
    a. magazine   c. road map
    b. dictionary   d. almanac

22. Two American spies have just been convicted. The best source of information about the sentences they received is __.
    a. a mystery book
    b. a newspaper
    c. an encyclopedia
    d. an almanac

23. The best source of information on the history of the Golden Retriever is __.
    a. an almanac
    b. an encyclopedia
    c. a newspaper
    d. a dictionary

24. Which source would you consult first to find articles about people who have won Oscar awards?
    a. newspaper
    b. almanac
    c. encyclopedia
    d. *Readers' Guide*

25. Which source would give the origin of the word *anorexia*?
    a. almanac   c. dictionary
    b. card catalog   d. atlas

READING COMPREHENSION

Directions: The purpose of this test is to find out how well you understand the materials you read. Read the selection first. Then read each item and decide which answer is correct or clearly better than the others. On your answer sheet, fill in the space that goes with the answer you choose.

The Japanese take their gardening very seriously. The *Kenrokuen*, for example, is a beautiful landscape garden created during the *Samurai* period (1676-1822). It contains almost 12,000 trees and shrubs which are always carefully tended.

For the Japanese people, the garden is a conscious effort to enhance nature. They do not put flowers and trees in patterns pleasing to the eye, as Westerners do. Instead, they try to arrange them as nature would, balancing the wild with the controlled. Irises, for instance, are planted by a stream and pebbles are combed into soothing waves. A black pine is pruned and trimmed carefully, not to make it resemble anything, but to highlight its trunk and limbs. A flowering shrub appears, not with others lining a walk, but by itself against a stone where its colors contrast with the black-gray of the rock.

The gardens are designed to be beautiful in winter, too. The white snow emphasizes the outline of the trees, especially that of the pine which they call "the king of trees." Delicate trees wear rice straw capes, and limbs of old trees are wrapped in webbing of gold-colored ropes to support them in the snow. There are no plastic covers or overturned flowerpots here; only artfully placed rocks and stark pebble walks to remind the beholder of the promise of spring.

---

1. The Japanese apparently __.
   a. are patient gardeners
   b. garden for their health
   c. have only public gardens
   d. grow trees for pleasure

2. The writer apparently __.
   a. prefers Western gardens
   b. admires Japanese gardens
   c. is overly critical of gardens
   d. dislikes bare gardens

3. Pruning is done to __.
   a. encourage growth
   b. prevent bark diseases
   c. emphasize form
   d. create pleasing shapes

4. Japanese gardens primarily __.
   a. grow food
   b. picture wild nature
   c. reflect on personal ideas
   d. magnify natural beauty

A *luthier* is someone who makes guitars. Like the violins in the day of Stradivari, guitars today are being made to meet the personal needs of guitarists, particularly the great players.

Unlike an electric guitar which is solid, the acoustic guitar is hollow. Its sound depends on the way the vibrating strings cause the sound board, the top of the instrument, to resonate with them. The luthier uses spruce wood, which is both strong and porous, so the sound can vibrate and pass through to the inside of the instrument where it bounces off the sides and back, then comes out again through the round opening in the center of the guitar.

Danny Ferrington is a luthier who makes guitars for some of the big name stars today. He is an unpretentious young man from the back country of Louisiana. He fell in love with the guitar when he was twelve years old and went to Nashville where he apprenticed for a guitar maker for the bluegrass singers. Then he went to Los Angeles where he has made guitars for Johnny Cash, Eric Clapton, Jackson Brown, and Linda Ronstadt. His guitars are asymmetrical and of varied shapes which he finds gives them a clearer sound for recording. The innovative shapes make it possible to create instruments as works of art, lovingly designed and crafted by the artist for another artist.

---

5. Spruce is a good wood for making guitars because it __.
   a. can withstand vibrations
   b. doesn't vibrate
   c. produces good sound
   d. is a natural substance

6. Great acoustic guitars do not have to be __.
   a. wood   c. symmetrical
   b. metal   d. porous

7. Apparently, Danny makes good guitars because __.
   a. he loves his work
   b. great artists buy them
   c. the author admires him
   d. he was trained in Nashville

8. Which of these is the best title for the passage?
   a. "The Great Luthier"
   b. "Danny Ferrington, the Luthier"
   c. "Sound and Motion"
   d. "How to Make a Guitar"

9. In the writer's opinion, guitar making is __.
   a. an art that takes talent
   b. an expensive hobby
   c. easy if you use the right materials
   d. a new industry

Swift Things Are Beautiful

1 Swift things are beautiful:
Swallows and deer,
3 And lightning that falls
Bright-veined and clear,
5 Rivers and meteors,
Wind in the wheat
7 The strong-withered horse,
The runner's sure feet.

9 And slow things are beautiful:
The closing of day,
11 The pause of the wave
That curves downward to spray,
13 The ember that crumbles,
The opening flower
15 And the ox that moves on
In the quiet of power.

Elizabeth Coatsworth

---

10. In *Line 4,* the phrase *bright-veined* refers to the __.
a. bloody look of lightning
b. flash of lightning
c. long, thin flash of lightning
d. heat of lightning

11. In *Line 7, withered* has the Old English meaning of "against." So, *strong-withered* means __.
a. against the rider
b. against the wagon
c. against time
d. against the wind

12. The poet says that "slow things are beautiful" because __.
a. she changed her mind
b. there are not enough beautiful swift things
c. she no longer admires swift things
d. all things are beautiful in her eyes

13. The slowest thing the poet mentions is __.
a. a wave   c. a flower
b. an ember   d. the day

A *spoonerism* is not the misuse of tableware. It occurs when you switch syllables or the letters of two or more words in a sentence. The results can be both funny and embarrassing.

Spoonerisms have been around since language became a means of communication. However, Dr. Archibald Spooner, a teacher at Oxford University in England and a clergyman as well, is the person who made them famous. Dr. Spooner suffered from nervousness and poor eyesight. This may have made it difficult for him to see words correctly and to repeat them accurately.

One time he accused a student of "kissing my mystery lecture" when he meant to say "missing my history lecture." He told another student that the young man had "deliberately tasted a worm and could leave Oxford by the town drain." He meant to say that the student had "wasted a term and could leave by the down train."

The medical term for this problem is *metathesis*, but people still call the bloopers spoonerisms. Try making them up. They're "feally run!"

14. Why did Dr. Spooner speak so strangely?
   a. He suffered from a disease.
   b. He wanted to be a comedian.
   c. He didn't approve of lectures.
   d. Poor students annoyed him.

15. Spoonerism involves ___.
   a. replacing words and phrases in a sentence
   b. eliminating syllables in a word
   c. using words with double meanings
   d. switching letters and syllables in a sentence

16. Which of these is the most appropriate title for the passage?
   a. "Silly Speech"
   b. "How to Sound Like a Teacher"
   c. "Table Manners for the Clergy"
   d. "Sounds and Syllables"

17. Apparently, Dr. Spooner ___.
   a. enjoyed insulting people
   b. wasn't as smart as he should have been
   c. didn't mean to embarrass anyone
   d. was insensitive and unkind

VOCABULARY

Directions: This test will show if you understand the meanings of different words and if you recognize words that have the same meaning. It will also show how well you can use context clues to define new words. Mark your answers on your answer sheet.

For items 1-10, choose the word or phrase that means the same, or almost the same, as the word in dark type.

1. to **enhance** the melody
   a. play
   b. recognize
   c. repeat
   d. improve

2. **legend** of Davy Crockett
   a. true story
   b. unverified story
   c. musical
   d. history

3. feel **devastated**
   a. happy
   b. calm
   c. upset
   d. betrayed

4. **redress** injustice
   a. hate
   b. resent
   c. create
   d. correct

5. **configuration** of circles and squares
   a. meeting
   b. drawing
   c. photo
   d. pattern

6. **cognizant** of his rights
   a. knowledgeable
   b. ignorant
   c. scared
   d. unaware

7. a **renewal** program
   a. health
   b. road
   c. rebuilding
   d. educational

8. a young **entrepreneur**
   a. teacher
   b. politician
   c. athlete
   d. innovator

9. arts **foundation**
   a. building
   b. cellar
   c. beginning
   d. organization

10. peanut **by-product**
    a. additional product
    b. waste product
    c. new product
    d. poisonous product

For items 11-20, read each incomplete sentence. Choose the word or phrase that best completes the sentence.

11. Viscous material is liquid but __.
    a. sweet
    b. non-flowing
    c. hot
    d. lumpy

12. A teaching fellow at a university is __.
    a. a member of the faculty
    b. the Dean's relative
    c. someone who can't be dismissed
    d. a favorite professor

13. A destitute family is __.
    a. lucky
    b. affectionate
    c. very poor
    d. new to the neighborhood

14. An advantageous time for moving is __.
    a. a good time
    b. a bad time
    c. a wrong time
    d. anytime

15. How well you studied is manifest in __.
    a. tests
    b. class discussions
    c. written reports
    d. all of the above

16. To disseminate gossip through the newspaper could __.
    a. result in a libel suit
    b. make money for you
    c. make you popular
    d. make someone feel good

17. To be unobtrusive is to be __.
    a. easily seen
    b. alone
    c. unnoticeable
    d. kind

18. To reiterate a warning is to __.
    a. state it clearly
    b. disown it
    c. shout it
    d. repeat it

19. Citizens without any autonomy are __.
    a. governed by a tyrant
    b. living in a democracy
    c. economically poor
    d. part of a republic

20. When you obliterate your record you __.
    a. repeat it
    b. erase it
    c. print it
    d. restudy it

For items 21-26, read the selection below. Notice the test words in dark type. Choose the word that best answers each question about the test words.

Many birds do not build nests. Falcons, for example, lay their eggs on the bare ground. Other birds find it easier to take over the abandoned nests of others. Starlings are **prone** to chase birds from their nests and then occupy the nest themselves. Sparrows, parrots, wrens, and purple martins also have this same **predilection** for laziness. Perhaps this is why they are more easily **domesticated** than wilder species like robins.

It is the more **stalwart** females, however, who do all the work among the species which do build nests. They build bowl-shaped structures of grass, twigs, and **remnants** of string, fabric, or anything they can find and carry in their beaks. Then they use a **viscous** substance which will eventually harden and hold the pieces together. Robins and bluebirds use mud while the hummingbird uses spider webs. Some birds who are easily frightened enclose their homes entirely, leaving only a tiny hole for an opening.

21. What does **prone** mean in the selection?
   a. lying flat   c. quick
   b. inclined to   d. slow

22. What does **predilection** mean in the selection?
   a. inclination   c. show
   b. hatred   d. fear

23. What does **domesticated** mean in the selection?
   a. caught   c. netted
   b. harmed   d. tamed

24. What does **stalwart** mean in the selection?
   a. lazy   c. faithful
   b. strong   d. female

25. What does **remnants** mean in the selection?
   a. scraps   c. pieces
   b. boxes   d. fabrics

26. What does **viscous** mean in the selection?
   a. sweet   c. dry
   b. sticky   d. cold

Directions: This test will show how well you can find and use information from maps, tables, graphs, and reference materials. Read each question. Four answer choices are given, but only one is correct. Fill in the space for the best answer on your answer sheet.

STRONG SHOWING OF WEAKFISH

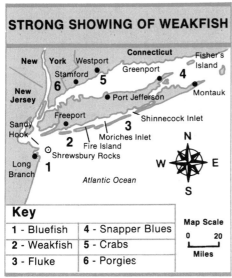

Key

1 - Bluefish	4 - Snapper Blues
2 - Weakfish	5 - Crabs
3 - Fluke	6 - Porgies

Map Scale
0   20
Miles

MORE OF ELDERLY VOTE

Age group	Number that voted (in millions)	Percentage
18-24	11.4	40.8%
25-29	10.7	50.8%
30-34	11.3	58.6%
35-39	10.6	62.4%
40-44	8.9	64.9%
45-49	7.5	65.8%
50-54	7.5	69.4%
55-59	8.1	72.2%
60-64	7.8	71.9%
65-69	6.6	72.8%
70+	11.5	65.1%

Source: Election Data Services Inc.

1. The best bluefishing is near __.
   a. Shrewsbury   c. Greenport
   b. Montauk   d. Stamford

2. Crabbing is the best near __.
   a. Westport
   b. Greenport
   c. the Moriches inlet
   d. Long Branch

3. Fishing for flukes would be best near __.
   a. Stamford   c. Shinnecock
   b. Shrewsbury   d. Freeport

4. For snapper blues, take your fishing rod to __.
   a. Fire Island   c. Freeport
   b. Sandy Hook   d. Montauk

5. Which age group has the most conscientious number of voters?
   a. 65-69   c. 18-24
   b. 70 and up   d. 30-34

6. Which age group has the highest percentage of voters?
   a. 65-69   c. 35-39
   b. 70 and up   d. 50-54

7. In which age group do half of the eligible voters vote?
   a. 45-49   c. 50-54
   b. 25-29   d. 30-34

8. The total eligible voters for ages 25-29 would be about __.
   a. 25,000,000   c. 11,000,000
   b. 30,000,000   d. 20,000,000

AUTOMOTIVE MARKET SHARE

July, 1985 (%)		July, 1986 (%)
21.3	Ford	21.1
10.3	Chrysler	11.6
2.1	A.M.C.	1.6
1.5	Volkswagen	1.4
2.9	Honda	3.9
6.2	Nissan	4.5
8.8	Toyota	8.9
2.1	Mazda	2.1
5.9	Other	8.6
	imports	

How market was divided in July, for domestic and imported cars and light trucks

General Motors 38.9%

General Motors 36.3%

MORE WOMEN GAINING SEATS IN LEGISLATURES

State	Percent	Rank	State	Percent	Rank
Ala.	6.4%	46	Mont.	14.7%	25
Alaska	18.3%	15	Neb.	16.3%	19
Ariz.	20.0%	8	Nev.	15.9%	21
Ark.	7.4%	42	N.H.	33.0%	1
Calif.	12.5%	30	N.J.	10.0%	36
Colo.	24.0%	4	N.M.	11.6%	33
Conn.	21.9%	7	N.Y.	10.9%	34
Del.	16.1%	20	N.C.	11.8%	32
Fla.	19.4%	10	N.D.	11.9%	31
Ga.	9.7%	37	Ohio	9.1%	38
Hawaii	18.4%	14	Okla.	8.7%	40
Idaho	19.1%	12	Ore.	20.0%	9
Ill.	16.9%	17	Pa.	5.1%	48
Ind.	12.7%	29	R.I.	15.3%	23
Iowa	14.7%	24	S.C.	5.8%	47
Kan.	18.2%	16	S.D.	14.3%	26
Ky.	6.5%	45	Tenn.	8.3%	41
La.	4.8%	49	Texas	8.8%	39
Maine	23.7%	6	Utah	6.7%	44
Md.	19.2%	11	Vt.	26.1%	2
Mass.	16.5%	18	Va.	7.1%	43
Mich.	10.8%	35	Wash.	23.8%	5
Minn.	13.9%	27	W.Va.	15.7%	22
Miss.	2.3%	50	Wis.	18.9%	13
Mo.	13.2%	28	Wyo.	25.6%	3

9. Which imported car had the biggest sale in July, 1985?
   a. Mazda
   c. Toyota
   b. Honda
   d. Nissan

10. Ford sales in July, 1985 was __ more than in July, 1986.
    a. 2%
    c. 2.2%
    b. 20%
    d. .2%

11. In July, 1986, other imports accounted for __ 10% of the total market share.
    a. less than
    c. exactly
    b. more than
    d. maybe

12. The circle graphs indicate more __ cars sold in July of each year.
    a. foreign
    c. Japanese
    b. GM
    d. American

13. __ has the highest percentage of women legislators.
    a. Ohio
    b. New Hampshire
    c. New Jersey
    d. California

14. __ has the lowest percentage of women legislators.
    a. Wyoming
    c. Florida
    b. Mississippi
    d. Arkansas

15. In how many states do women hold less than 10% of the seats in the legislature?
    a. 18
    c. 8
    b. 10
    d. 14

16. In how many states do women hold more than 25% of the seats in the legislature?
    a. 3
    c. 4
    b. 1
    d. 2

LIFE SAVING AND WATER SAFETY

INDEX

Lifeguard, 31, 96

Resuscitation, 118, 125-129, 199

Saddle back carry, 147
Safety equipment, 23-26, 67, 143-147
Scissors kick, 130
Shock in near drowning, 160-162, see also Resuscitation
Small craft safety, 54, 136-149
Sunstroke, 158
Surfboard, 34-36, *see also* Undertow

Tired Swimmer Carry, 40-41

Undertow, 180
Underwater approach, 104-105

17. On which pages would you find information about saving an exhausted swimmer?
    a. 34-36   c. 143-147
    b. 40-41   d. 136-149

18. What pages give information on managing small boats?
    a. 136-149   c. 143-147
    b. 104-105   d. 136-149

19. What pages discuss lifesaving procedures?
    a. 34, 35   c. 41, 118, 199
    b. 143, 158   d. 67, 180, 198

20. The dangers of an undertow are discussed on pages __.
    a. 125-129, 104
    b. 34, 35, 36, 180
    c. 136, 137, 158
    d. 23, 24, 25, 147

Directions: Answer questions 21-25 about reference materials.

21. To find information on how to prepare for a job interview, first consult __.
    a. an encyclopedia
    b. *Readers' Guide*
    c. the almanac
    d. a newspaper

22. You have a job offer in Oregon. To know its current population, consult __.
    a. a newspaper
    b. a dictionary
    c. an almanac
    d. an encyclopedia

23. The job involves electronics. To read about this industry, first consult the card catalog and __.
    a. an almanac
    b. a telephone directory
    c. a newspaper
    d. *Readers' Guide*

24. For information on the best roads into Oregon, consult __.
    a. an almanac
    b. an encyclopedia
    c. *Readers' Guide*
    d. an atlas

25. To find an apartment in Oregon, consult __.
    a. an almanac
    b. an atlas
    c. a local newspaper
    d. a magazine

Vocabulary Glossary

Here are the new words and their meanings, which you have learned in the vocabulary lessons. Remember, sometimes a word can have more than one meaning. The meanings listed here fit the way the words were used in the passages you read.

abnormal — not normal or unusual
acclaimed — praised
acumen — sharpness and skill
advantageous — fortunate
aerated — exposed to air
agitation — violent movement
alienate — to make unfriendly or disunite
alleged — so-called
alleviate — lighten or relieve
alter — change
amber — deep yellow
anonymity — being unknown
anticipating — expecting
apartheid — segregation
appreciation — gratitude
apprehensive — anxious
attest — prove
auspices — sponsorship
autonomous — self-governing

bicentennial — occurring every two hundred years
blanket — soft, warm covering
blemish — defect or imperfection
blessing — approving expression
bravado — pretended courage
by-products — additional things

canteen — covered water bottle
capability — skill
celestial — heavenly or in the sky
cognizant — knowledgeable

collide — clash or crash together
commitments — promises
competent — capable or skilled
composed — calm
configuration — pattern
conspicuous — visible
constraining — restricting
crimp — to crumple or to restrain
cultivated — grown
curiosity — something odd

debilitating — weakening
debunk — expose as false
decomania — mad about art deco
deprecating — disapproving
depression — period of economic trouble
destitute — very poor
devastated — ruined
disassociate — separate in the mind
disavowal — denial
discount — disregard
disparate — different
dispatch — send off
dissembling — disguising
disseminated — spread
distraught — bewildered or agitated
diverse — different
diversification — variation
diversity — variety
domesticated — tamed

enchanting — fascinating

endeavor — attempt or to try
enhanced — improved
entrepreneur — originator
ethereal — out of this world
exempt — free or excused
extraordinary — highly unusual

favored — preferred
favor — small gift
feedback — reaction
feigned — pretended
fellow — comrade or associate
formal — ceremonial or orderly
foundation — organization
frugality — thriftiness

grip — hold firmly
gull — fool or trick
gullible — believing (anything)

harmony — pleasing sounds
harried — hurried or worried
heed — follow
heterogeneous — dissimilar
hoopla — commotion
hues — colors

impressionable — easily influenced
inaccessible — impossible to reach
incomprehensible — not
    understandable
incontestable — proven
indigenous — native
induce — cause
ingenious — clever
inhibited — fearful or unresponsive
initiated — introduced or began
initiative — own effort
innocence — simple nature
innovation — new idea
inscrutable — mysterious
insensitive — not caring

interfaith — of different religions
international — between nations
intricate — complicated

launch — set off
legend — extraordinary person or
    unverified story
legumes — plants producing
    edible seeds
loner — unsociable person
lumbering — walking clumsily

magazine — a periodical
malevolent — evil
manifest — evident or seen
masticate — chew
melancholy — sadness or gloom
menace — threat
minimize — make little
monopolizing — dominating
moor — inhabitant of Morocco
multishaped — having many shapes
musicologist — one who studies
    music

necessitates — requires
negate — to deny
negative — unfavorable
nomenclature — name
novel — new

obligations — duties
obliterated — erased or removed
obnoxious — hateful
origins — beginnings

paraphernalia — equipment
passage — journey
pensive — thoughtful
perceptible — can be detected
permeating — going through
perplexities — confusions

phenomenon — strange happening
plague — cause trouble
pragmatic — useful or practical
predilection — a taste or liking
present — gift
prestigious — impressive
prevalent — common
profoundly — deeply
prone — inclined
protract — to prolong
provoke — to stimulate or stir up
psychic — spiritualistic

quintessential — most typical

race — a competition
radical — revolutionist or extremist
raft — wooden craft for riding on
    water
raging — spreading
rare — unusual
recreating — refreshing
redress — correct or make right
reflect — think or meditate
rehabilitation — reeducation
reiterates — repeats
relax — become less stiff or loosen
remnants — remainders or leftovers
renewal — restoration or reform
reprehensible — not admirable
requisite — necessary
requite — repay
resin — gum or sap
restitution — reparation or payment
revered — honored
revolutionize — change
rigid — stiff or inflexible

sage — wise person
seal — arctic animal
selective — careful about choosing

significant — important
skinning — removing the skin
    from something
stalwart — fearless
stereotype — fixed impression
stories — floors in a building
strand — beach
subjected (to) — caused to undergo
superseded — went beyond
surmised — guessed

tampered — meddled
tentatively — hesitantly
therapy — treatment
thrive — grow
tidbit — morsel
tissues — group of living cells
title — legal proof of ownership of
    property
tolerance — endurance or open-
    mindedness
toll — sound of a bell
trackless — not on tracks

unassuming — modest or humble
unctuous — rich in fat and oil
unique — one of a kind
unobtrusive — unnoticeable
unpretentious — plain or modest
unverified — unproven

vibrate — to quiver
viscous — non-flowing
visualize — imagine
vitalized — made energetic or
    lively
vulgarism — coarse or crude
    remark

waspish — mean and sharp-
    tongued

Answer Key

UNIT I READING COMPREHENSION

Pages 14–15: 1. d, 2. d, 3. c, 4. c, 5. a, 6. d

Pages 16–17: 1. c, 2. a, 3. b, 4. c, 5. d

Pages 18–19: 1. a, 2. c, 3. d, 4. d, 5. d, 6. b

Pages 20–21: 1. a, 2. d, 3. c, 4. b, 5. d, 6. d

Pages 22–23: 1. c, 2. b, 3. d, 4. a, 5. c, 6. a

Pages 24–25: 1. d, 2. a, 3. d, 4. d, 5. c, 6. c

Page 26: 1. b, 2. b, 3. a, 4. a

Page 27: 5. c, 6. b, 7. b, 8. c, 9. c

Page 28: 10. b, 11. d, 12. b, 13. a, 14. d

Page 29: 15. b, 16. c, 17. a, 18. a, 19. b, 20. a

Pages 36–37: 1. b, 2. d, 3. d, 4. d, 5. d, 6. c

Pages 38–39: 1. b, 2. b, 3. d, 4. b, 5. d, 6. d

Pages 40–41: 1. d, 2. d, 3. d, 4. c, 5. b, 6. d

Pages 42–43: 1. b, 2. c, 3. c, 4. b, 5. c, 6. c

Pages 44–45: 1. a, 2. b, 3. a, 4. d, 5. a, 6. d

Page 46: 1. b, 2. c, 3. a, 4. d

Page 47: 1. b, 2. d, 3. b, 4. d, 5. a

Pages 48–49: 1. c, 2. b, 3. c, 4. d, 5. b, 6. d

Pages 50–51: 1. b, 2. c, 3. b, 4. a, 5. b, 6. c

Pages 52–53: 1. b, 2. b, 3. d, 4. c, 5. b, 6. c

Pages 54–56: 1. c, 2. c, 3. c, 4. d, 5. d, 6. b, 7. b, 8. c

Page 57: 1. b, 2. a, 3. a, 4. c

Page 58: 5. b, 6. c, 7. a, 8. d, 9. c, 10. a

Page 59: 11. c, 12. c, 13. b, 14. c, 15. b

Pages 66–67: 1. b, 2. d, 3. c, 4. d, 5. b

Pages 68–69: 1. d, 2. c, 3. c, 4. b, 5. c, 6. d

Pages 70–71: 1. d, 2. b, 3. d, 4. c, 5. d

Pages 72–73: 1. d, 2. d, 3. b, 4. c, 5. a

Pages 74–75: 1. c, 2. b, 3. a, 4. c, 5. b

Page 76: 1. d, 2. a, 3. c, 4. b

Page 77: 5. a, 6. c, 7. d, 8. c, 9. a

Page 78: 10. b, 11. b, 12. d, 13. a

UNIT II VOCABULARY

Pages 84–85: **A.** 1. entrepreneur, 2. resin, 3. masticate, 4. enhanced, 5. attest, 6. viscous, 7. initiated, 8. pragmatic; **B.** 1. c, 2. a, 3. b, 4. c

Pages 86–87: **A.** 1. fellow, 2. foundation, 3. diversification, 4. revolutionize, 5. unassuming, 6. destitute, 7. by-products, 8. acclaimed; **B.** 1. c, 2. b, 3. a, 4. c

Pages 88–89: **A.** 1. hues, 2. advantageous, 3. prevalent, 4. phenomenon, 5. Celestial, 6. manifest, 7. profoundly, 8. collide; **B.** 1. b, 2. c, 3. b, 4. a

Pages 90–91: **A.** 1. disseminated, 2. devastated, 3. cultivated, 4. surmise, 5. loner, 6. unverified, 7. domesticated, 8. legend; **B.** 1. a, 2. c, 3. b, 4. a

Pages 92–94: **A.** 1. heed, 2. feedback, 3. monopolizing, 4. menace, 5. obnoxious, 6. competent, 7. bravado, 8. deprecating, 9. blemish, 10. reiterates ; **B.** 1. c, 2. b, 3. a, 4. b

UNIT II VOCABULARY (Concluded)

Page 95: 1. viscous, 2. initiated, 3. revolutionized, 4. acclaimed, 5. manifest, 6. hues, 7. legends, 8. cultivated, 9. competent, 10. bravado

Pages 98–99: **A.** 1. unique, 2. incontestable, 3. cognizant, 4. disavowal, 5. configuration, 6. redress, 7. alleged, 8. tampered; **B.** 1. b, 2. a, 3. c, 4. a

Pages 100–101: **A.** 1. enchanting, 2. ingenious, 3. intricate, 4. malevolent, 5. significant, 6. gullible, 7. feigned, 8. dissembling; **B.** 1. a, 2. c, 3. a, 4. b

Pages 102–104: **A.** 1. obliterated, 2. anonymity, 3. restitution, 4. rehabilitation, 5. debunk, 6. autonomous, 7. unobtrusive, 8. psychic, 9. renewal, 10. hoopla; **B.** 1. b, 2. b, 3. a, 4. a, 5. b, 6. b

Page 105: 1. one of a kind, ordinary, 2. patterns, scatterings, 3. unquestionable, unproved, 4. clever, stupid, 5. believing, doubting, 6. complicated, simple, 7. reform, ruin, 8. self-governing, subordinate, 9. commotion, quiet, 10. unknownness, fame

Page 106: 1. b, 2. c, 3. a, 4. d, 5. b, 6. c, 7. d, 8. d, 9. a, 10. b

Page 107: 11. c, 12. a, 13. d, 14. b, 15. d, 16. a, 17. c, 18. b, 19. a, 20. d

Page 108: 21. d, 22. a, 23. a, 24. c, 25. c, 26. b, 27. c, 28. b, 29. c, 30. b

Page 109: 31. d, 32. a, 33. c, 34. a, 35. d, 36. c, 37. c, 38. a, 39. d, 40. a

Pages 114–115: **A.** 1. a, 2. c, 3. a, 4. a, 5. a, 6. a, 7. a, 8. c; **B.** prone—inclined, alienate—make unfriendly, aerate—exposed to air, alleviate—relieve, vitalized—lively, reflect—think, pensive—thoughtful, harried—hurried

Pages 116–117: **A.** 1. a, 2. a, 3. b, 4. a, 5. b, 6. c, 7. b, 8. a; **B.** unpretentious—modest, superseded—went beyond, perplexities—confusions, subjected (to)—caused to undergo, incomprehensible—not understandable, debilitating—weakening, visualize—imagine, therapy—treatment

Pages 118–119: **A.** 1. b, 2. b, 3. b, 4. a, 5. c, 6. a, 7. c, 8. c; **B.** harmony—pleasing sounds, novel—new, ethereal—strange and heavenly, predilection—preference, melancholy—sad, vibrate—quiver, inscrutable—mysterious, disparate—different

Pages 120–121: **A.** 1. b, 2. b, 3. a, 4. c, 5. a, 6. c, 7. c, 8. a; **B.** tentatively—hesitantly, interfaith—of different religions, endeavor—try, stereotype—fixed impression, inhibited—fearful, diversity—variety, apartheid—separateness, tolerance—open-mindedness

Page 122: 1. alienate, 2. pensive, 3. harried, 4. superseded, 5. unpretentious, 6. perplexities, 7. vibrate, 8. inscrutable, 9. interfaith, 10. endeavor

Page 123: 1. b, 2. b, 3. a, 4. c, 5. a, 6. a, 7. b, 8. b, 9. a, 10. d

Page 124: 11. b, 12. c, 13. c, 14. c, 15. a, 16. c, 17. d, 18. a

Page 125: 19. b, 20. c, 21. c, 22. b, 23. a, 24. d

Pages 130–131: **A.** 1. a, 2. a, 3. b, 4. b, 5. b, 6. a, 7. a, 8. b; **B.** 1. stalwart, 2. paraphernalia, 3. launch, 4. plague

Pages 132–133: **A.** 1. a, 2. b, 3. a, 4. a, 5. b, 6. b, 7. b, 8. b; **B.** 1. rare, 2. lumbering, 3. innocence, 4. appreciation

Pages 134–135: **A.** 1. b, 2. a, 3. a, 4. a, 5. a, 6. b, 7. b, 8. b, 9. a, 10. a; **B.** 1. gull, 2. race, 3. sage, 4. rigid

Page 136: 1. dispatch, 2. paraphernalia, 3. plague, 4. amber, 5. appreciation, 6. innocence, 7. rare, 8. sage, 9. unctuous, 10. rigid

Page 137: 1. b, 2. b, 3. b, 4. b, 5. b, 6. b, 7. b, 8. b

Pages 142–143: **A.** 1. a, 2. c, 3. b, 4. a, 5. c, 6. a, 7. a, 8. c

Pages 144–145: **A.** 1. b, 2. a, 3. b, 4. a, 5. a, 6. c, 7. b, 8. c

Page 146: 1. d, 2. b, 3. c, 4. d, 5. b, 6. d, 7. c, 8. b

Project Achievement: Reading — Book H

UNIT III   STUDY SKILLS

Page 149: 1. a, 2. b, 3. c, 4. d
Page 151: 1. b, 2. d, 3. a, 4. a, 5. d, 6. b, 7. a, 8. b
Page 153: 1. c, 2. a, 3. d, 4. a, 5. b, 6. d, 7. a, 8. a
Page 155: 1. a, 2. d, 3. b, 4. d, 5. d, 6. a, 7. b, 8. b
Page 157: 1. c, 2. a, 3. d, 4. a, 5. c, 6. a, 7. c, 8. b
Page 159: 1. a, 2. b, 3. b, 4. a, 5. c, 6. a, 7. a, 8. d
Page 161: 1. b, 2. b, 3. b, 4. d, 5. b, 6. d, 7. d, 8. c
Page 163: 1. c, 2. a, 3. a, 4. b, 5. a, 6. b, 7. b, 8. d
Page 165: 1. b, 2. a, 3. b, 4. b, 5. a, 6. d, 7. b, 8. b
Page 167: 1. b, 2. c, 3. a, 4. b, 5. b, 6. a, 7. a, 8. d
Page 169: 1. b, 2. d, 3. b, 4. b, 5. a, 6. c, 7. b, 8. a
Page 170: 1. b, 2. c, 3. a, 4. a, 5. b, 6. b
Page 171: 7. a, 8. a, 9. d, 10. d, 11. d, 12. a
Page 172: 13. b, 14. a, 15. a, 16. d, 17. d, 18. d

Page 173: 19. a, 20. b, 21. c, 22. d, 23. c, 24. b
Page 175: 1. b, 2. b, 3. d
Page 177: 1. a, 2. b, 3. d, 4. b, 5. d, 6. c, 7. c, 8. c
Page 179: 1. d, 2. b, 3. b, 4. c, 5. a, 6. d, 7. d, 8. b
Page 181: 1. b, 2. d, 3. b, 4. c, 5. d, 6. d, 7. a, 8. b
Page 183: 1. c, 2. a, 3. b, 4. c, 5. d, 6. c, 7. c, 8. d
Page 185: 1. b, 2. b, 3. d, 4. a, 5. c, 6. a, 7. d, 8. b
Page 187: 1. c, 2. b, 3. c, 4. d, 5. d, 6. c, 7. b, 8. b
Page 189: 1. c, 2. c, 3. b, 4. c, 5. d, 6. a, 7. c, 8. a
Page 191: 1. d, 2. c, 3. a, 4. c, 5. b, 6. d, 7. a, 8. a
Page 193: 1. c, 2. c, 3. c, 4. a, 5. c, 6. c, 7. d, 8. b
Page 194: 1. b, 2. c, 3. d, 4. d, 5. d, 6. b, 7. d,
Page 195: 8. d, 9. b, 10. c, 11. d, 12. b, 13. a
Page 196: 14. c, 15. b, 16. c, 17. d, 18. a, 19. b, 20. c, 21. b, 22. d, 23. c

UNIT IV   TESTS

TEST 1
Reading Comprehension (pages 198–201): 1. d, 2. b, 3. a, 4. c, 5. c, 6. a, 7. b, 8. c, 9. a, 10. b, 11. c, 12. c, 13. b, 14. c, 15. c, 16. c, 17. d, 18. d
Vocabulary (pages 202–204): 1. b, 2. b, 3. a, 4. b, 5. c, 6. b, 7. c, 8. b, 9. c, 10. c, 11. c, 12. b, 13. a, 14. a, 15. c, 16. c, 17. a, 18. d, 19. b, 20. a, 21. b, 22. b, 23. a, 24. a, 25. c, 26. b, 27. b, 28. b
Study Skills (pages 205–207): 1. a, 2. a, 3. b, 4. b, 5. b, 6. a, 7. d, 8. d, 9. d, 10. a, 11. d, 12. c, 13. d, 14. a, 15. b, 16. b, 17. b, 18. a, 19. d, 20. a, 21. c, 22. b, 23. b, 24. d, 25. c

TEST 2
Reading Comprehension (pages 208–211): 1. a, 2. b, 3. c, 4. d, 5. a, 6. c, 7. b, 8. b, 9. a, 10. c, 11. d, 12. d, 13. c, 14. a, 15. d, 16. a, 17. c
Vocabulary (pages 212–214): 1. d, 2. b, 3. c, 4. d, 5. d, 6. a, 7. c, 8. d, 9. d, 10. a, 11. b, 12. a, 13. c, 14. a, 15. d, 16. a, 17. c, 18. d, 19. a, 20. b, 21. b, 22. a, 23. d, 24. b, 25. a, 26. b
Study Skills (pages 215–217): 1. a, 2. a, 3. c, 4. d, 5. b, 6. a, 7. b, 8. d, 9. c, 10. d, 11. a, 12. b, 13. b, 14. b, 15. d, 16. a, 17. b, 18. a, 19. c, 20 b, 21. b, 22. c, 23. d, 24. d, 25. c

PHOTO AND ART CREDITS